LEARNING ENGLISH

GREEN LINE NEW 1

Ausgabe für Bayern

WORKBOOK

von

Wolfgang Funk
Geraldine Greenhalgh
Marion Horner
Robert Parr
Dieter Prankel

Ernst Klett Verlag
Stuttgart Düsseldorf Leipzig

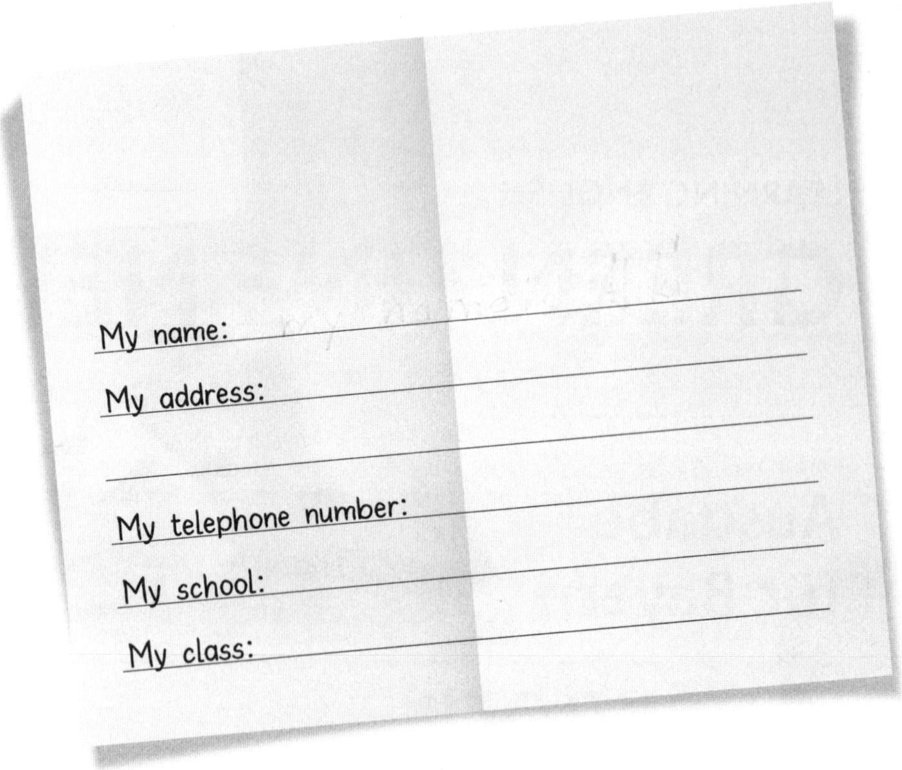

Ganz hinten im Heft findest du die Lösungen zu den Aufgaben der *Let's check*- und *Revision*-Seiten. Damit kannst du selber deine Arbeit überprüfen. Aber erst die Übungen bearbeiten, dann nachschauen!

Diese Arbeitsanweisungen findest du immer wieder in diesem *Workbook*. Falls du dir mal nicht ganz sicher bist, was du tun sollst, kannst du in dieser Liste nachschauen.

Ask your partner. [ˌɑːsk jɔː ˈpɑːtnə]	Frage deinen Partner.
Be ready to talk about this in class. [bi ˌredi tə ˈtɔːk‿əbaʊt ðɪs‿ɪn ˌklɑːs]	Bereite dich darauf vor, darüber im Unterricht zu sprechen.
Colour in … [ˌkʌlər‿ˈɪn]	Male … an.
Connect … [kəˈnekt]	Verbinde …
Cross out … [ˌkrɒs‿ˈaʊt]	Streiche … durch.
Crossword [ˈkrɒswɜːd]	Kreuzworträtsel
Exchange … [ɪksˈtʃeɪndʒ]	Tausche … aus
Fill in … [ˌfɪl‿ˈɪn]	Setze … ein. / Fülle … aus.
Finish … [ˈfɪnɪʃ]	Beende …
In English [ɪn‿ˈɪŋglɪʃ]	Auf Englisch
In German [ɪn ˈdʒɜːmən]	Auf Deutsch
Let's talk about … [lets ˈtɔːk‿əˌbaʊt]	Lasst uns über … sprechen.
Make notes. [ˌmeɪk ˈnəʊts]	Mache dir Notizen.
Match the sound pairs. [ˌmætʃ ðə ˈsaʊnd peəz]	Suche die passenden Lautpaare.
Opposites [ˈɒpəzɪts]	Gegensätze
Put in the right words/forms. [pʊt‿ɪn ðə ˈraɪt ˌwɜːdz/ˌfɔːmz]	Setze die richtigen Wörter / Formen ein.
Questions and answers [ˌkwestʃənz‿n‿ˈɑːntsəz]	Fragen und Antworten
Say it in English. [ˌseɪ‿ɪt‿ɪn‿ˈɪŋglɪʃ]	Sage es auf Englisch.
Sounds and spelling [ˌsaʊndz‿n ˈspelɪŋ]	Laute und Rechtschreibung
Underline … [ˌʌndəˈlaɪn]	Unterstreiche …
What are the words? [ˌwɒt‿ɑː ðə ˈwɜːdz]	Kennst du die Wörter?
Write about … [ˈraɪt‿əˌbaʊt]	Schreibe über …

1 Hello

1 Hello (Ausschneidebogen 1, PB p. 8/9)

Fill in.

1. Hello. My name is ______ Dixon.
I'm ______.
______ from ______.

2. Hi. I'm ______ Croft.
I'm ______ and I'm
______ London. ______
new ______ Nottingham.

2 My name is … (PB p. 9)

Fill in.

And you? What's ______ your
______? ______
old ______ you? ______
are you ______?

You:

______ ______ is
______ ______.
I'm ______.
______ from ______.

You

2 Friends

1 Make sentences (PB p. 11 / ex. 3)

1. my • Becky • is • This • best • She's • friend

   Sarah: This is Becky. She's my best friend.

2. Becky • Robert • I'm • Croft • Hi

   Robert: ______________________________

3. is • from • new • Robert • here • London • He's

   Sarah: ______________________________

4. His • Barker • dog • my • is • This • is • name

   Becky: ______________________________

5. School • new • Haywood • my • school • is

   Robert: ______________________________

6. That's • my • He's • in • too • tutor • David • group

   Sarah: ______________________________

2 Write about your best friends (PB p. 11 / ex. 4)

Your friend

__________ name __________

______________________________.

__________'s __________.

__________'s from

______________________________.

__________ name __________

______________________________.

__________'s __________.

__________'s from

______________________________.

Your friend

3 Crossword (PB p. 11 / ex. 2)

1. Robert is new →**1**.
2. *Sarah:* Tabby is my →**2**.
3. Let's go. →**3**, Becky.
4. *Robert:* Hello, dog.
   Barker: →**4**.
5. Becky is at ↓**8** →**5**.
6. *Sarah:* She's in my →**6**.
7. *Becky:* Barker is my →**7**.

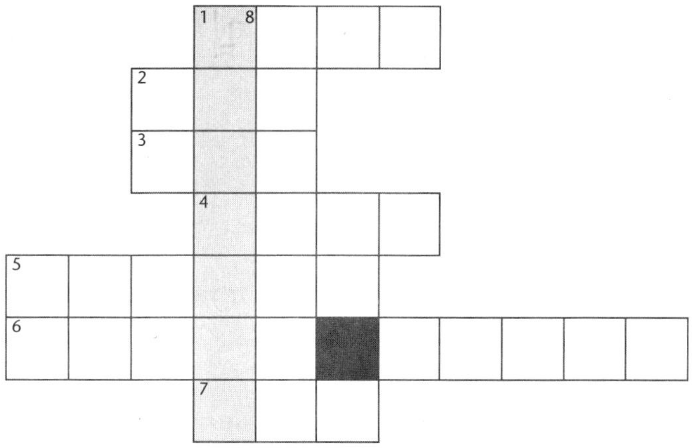

4 Numbers (PB p. 11 / ex. 5)

Write the numbers.

1. You say [fɔː], you write four.
2. You say [eɪt], you write ______.
3. You say [tuː], you write ______.
4. You say [wʌn], you write ______.
5. You say [naɪn], you write ______.
6. You say [faɪv], you write ______.
7. You say [θriː], you write ______.
8. You say ['sevn], you write ______.
9. You say [ten], you write ______.
10. You say [sɪks], you write ______.

5 What are the words? (PB p. 11 / ex. 6)

1. TW ______

2. ______

3. ______

4. ______

3 David and Robert

1 Short or long forms? (PB p. 12 / ex. 1)

am / 'm   are / 're   are not / aren't   is / 's   is not / isn't

1. That isn't my exercise book! My exercise book ______ here.
2. Where ______ my skates? They ______ here!
3. No, this ______ our tutor group.
4. Barker ______ a cat. He ______ a dog.
5. I ______ new in Nottingham, but you ______.
6. David and Sarah ______ in one tutor group, but they ______ best friends.

2 What's missing? (PB p. 12 / ex. 2)

1. How old is Robert? – He's twelve.
2. Is Sarah at Hogwood school? – No. ______ at Haywood School.
3. Is Haywood School in London? – No. ______ in Nottingham.
4. Is Mr Cooper nice? – Er, ______ OK.
5. Is Barker a cat? – ______.

3 Our friends from Nottingham (PB p. 12 / ex. 3)

my   your   his   her   our   your   their

1. I'm Robert. Becky, Sarah and David are ______ new friends.
2. We're new in Nottingham. That's ______ house over there.
3. Wow! I like ______ skates, David.
4. Hi, girls. Is that ______ school?
5. That's Sarah, and that's ______ cat Tabby.
6. Becky, Sarah and David are at Haywood School. I'm in ______ tutor group.
7. That's Barker. Is Tabby ______ friend?

4 Sound practice (PB p. 13 / ex. 5)

Put in the words. best bye five friend girl her hurt nice twelve

[aɪ]	[ɜː]	[e]

5 What colour are they? (PB p. 13 / ex. 7)

Colour in the things: ***red, yellow, green, blue, pink, brown, orange, purple, black.***

And now ask your partner:
Example: What colour is your cat? – My cat is black. Go on.

6 Say it in English: Hello (PB p. 13)

1. Hallo, wie geht es dir? – Danke, mir geht's gut. ______________________

2. Wo kommst du her? – Ich komme aus Nottingham. ______________________

3. Ist das Sarah? – Ja, sie ist meine beste Freundin. ______________________

4. Ich mag deine Rollschuhe. – Ja, sie sind wirklich schnell. ______________________

5. Bist du verletzt? – Nein, alles in Ordnung. ______________________

4 Robert! Where are your school things?

1 Sound practice (PB p. 14/ex. 2)

Make lists. books bags biros cats comics sentences drawers exercises groups houses names pencil cases schools skates

[s]	[z]	[ɪz]
____	____	____
____	____	____
____	____	____
____	____	____
____	____	

Tipp
Wie du schon erkannt hast, kann ein Buchstabe im Englischen für mehrere Laute stehen.
Wenn du nicht weißt, wie ein Wort ausgesprochen wird, schaue in das Wörterverzeichnis (Seite 156).
Die so genannte „phonetische Lautschrift" zeigt dir, wie das Wort ausgesprochen wird.
Nützlich, nicht wahr?

2 Find the things (PB p. 14/ex. 4)

~~R~~	~~U~~	~~L~~	~~E~~	~~R~~	Q	R	E	C
M	A	W	X	U	T	Z	N	O
A	F	A	E	B	A	S	P	M
G	O	T	R	B	L	R	E	P
A	L	Z	C	E	P	E	N	U
Z	D	B	I	R	O	U	C	T
I	E	B	S	K	L	Y	I	E
N	R	R	E	D	C	X	L	R
E	Z	D	B	F	G	E	C	H
V	H	C	O	M	I	C	R	T
S	C	H	O	O	L	B	A	G
B	O	O	K	I	B	P	E	I
A	G	B	L	E	W	T	Q	R

→
1. ruler
2. ____
3. ____
4. ____
5. ____
6. ____
7. ____

↓
1. ____
2. ____
3. ____
4. ____
5. ____
6. ____

3 Where are the things? (PB p. 15/ex. 5)

a) Look at the picture and put in: on under next to in

1. Where's the pen? It's on the folder.
2. Where are the football magazines?

They're ____________ the ____________

3. Where ____________

____________ the desk.

4. Where ____________

____

5. Where ____________

____

6. Where ____________

____

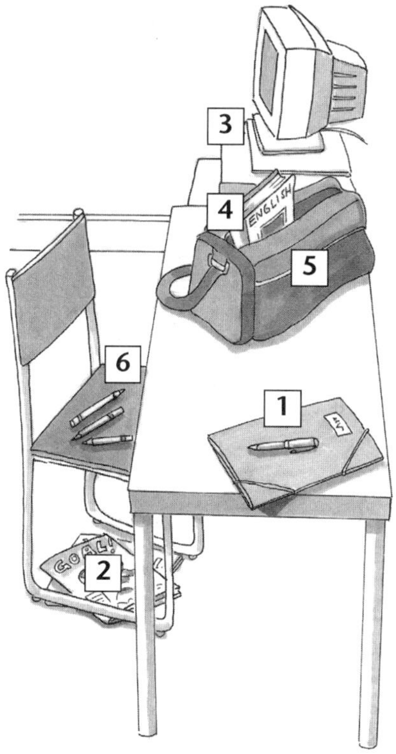

b) Make sentences with *there's/there are.*

There's a pen on the folder.

____

____

____

____

____

4 *This/that – these/those* (PB p. 15/ex. 9)

This is a pen and that's a rubber.

____

____

____

____

____

5 School!

1 The teachers (PB p. 16/ex. 1)

Put in the right words.

Robert: 7MD? What_____'s that?

Sarah: Our t_____ g_____, s_____!

Robert: And w_____'s our tutor?

Becky: Mrs Dane. S_____ our English teacher_____, too.

Robert: And w_____ a_____ the t_____ here?
A_____ t_____ OK?

Becky: The teachers? Yes, t_____ OK.

David: Mr Cooper is our G_____ t_____. He's n_____!

Sarah: Are you g_____ a_____ German, Robert?

Robert: No, I_____!

2 Robert and his skates (PB p. 17/ex. 3)

Put in: my your your your you're his he's they're they're aren't aren't there where where

Robert Croft is new at Haywood School. _____ good at skating[1]. _____ skates _____ new, but _____ really fast. But _____ are they now?

Robert: Mum, _____ are _____ skates? They _____ in my room.

Mrs Croft: _____ skates? _____ over _____, under _____ bed!

Robert: Thanks, Mum. _____ really nice!

Mrs Croft: Oh dear, Robert. Look at _____ room!

[1] ['skeɪtɪŋ] – Rollschuhlaufen

Tipp

Markiere die *short forms* auf dieser Doppelseite in Farbe. Dann kannst du später immer zurückblättern, wenn du schnell nachschauen möchtest – und die *short forms* fallen dir sofort auf.

3 What's in the room? (PB p. 17 / ex. 6)

a) Fill in the crossword

b) Now write six sentences about the room.

1. There's a computer on the desk.

4 Answer the questions (PB p. 17 / ex. 6)

1. Are you 11? ______
2. Are you from Nottingham? ______
3. Is your best friend German? ______
4. Is your best friend good at Maths? ______
5. Are you good at everything? ______
6. Who is your English teacher? ______
7. Is your English teacher English? ______

6 Pictures in the classroom

1 Questions and short answers (PB p. 18 / ex. 2)

1. Is that your football magazine, David? – Yes, ________
2. ________, Mrs. Dane? – No, ________
3. ________ your best ________, Sarah? – ________
4. ________ those ________? – ________
5. ________? – ________
6. ________ Robert new at Haywood School? – ________
7. ________ Becky and Sarah from London? – ________
8. ________ Barker your dog, Becky? – ________

2 Match the sound pairs (PB p. 18 / ex. 2)

hurt don't blue really Maths ~~laugh~~

maybe where floor please Barker rubber

class [ɑː] – laugh	funny [ʌ] –	bag [æ] –
game [eɪ] –	chair [eə] –	drawer [ɔː] –
folder [əʊ] –	who [uː] –	these [iː] –
hear [ɪə] –	answer [ɑː] –	girl [ɜː] –

3 Short answers (PB p. 19 / ex. 5)

Put in the short answers.

That's a terrible picture! – No, it isn't!

The colours aren't nice. – ______

The girl is too old. – ______

Her nose is too long. – ______

Her hands are funny. – ______

Is it a famous picture? – ______. It's the *Mona Lisa*!

4 Let's talk about their pictures (PB p. 19 / ex. 6)

What's missing? Put in the right word or words.

Becky: ______ that your picture, David?

David: Yes, ______.

Becky: ______ brilliant. I like ______ colours. And ______ those your skates ______ the picture?

David: Yes, ______. But I like the things in ______ picture over there! Is that ______ picture, Robert?

Robert: Yes, ______. But ______ a terrible picture!

Sarah: ______ say that, Robert. It's funny, but it ______ terrible!

Becky: Hey, ______ at ______ picture here! Ha, ha! ______ very funny.

Sarah: ______ too loud! ______ my picture!

Becky: Oh dear! But I like the monsters! ______ so nice.

Sarah: Monsters? ______ aren't monsters, ______ cats, silly!

Tipp

Hier noch ein Tipp: Wenn du zu Hause einen festen Arbeitsplatz für deine Hausaufgaben hast, dann mach dir bitte ein kleines Poster mit den Lang- und Kurzformen und hänge es in der Nähe deines Arbeitsplatzes an die Wand. Überlege mit einem Partner oder einer Partnerin, wie man diese Formen am besten ordnen kann.

7 The lesson

1 A lesson with Mr Gray (PB p. 21 / ex. 2)

Put in the words.

Mr Gray: Good morning ________ (**nimrong**), boys and ________ (**lirgs**). I'm your new Maths ________ (**chertea**). My name is Gray.

Becky: Can you ________ (**lespl**) your name, ________ (**elaspe**), Mr Gray?

Mr Gray: Yes. It's G-R-**A-Y** – not E-Y like the ________ (**roculo**)! Here are your Maths ________ (**bosko**). Let's start the ________ (**nossel**) on ________ (**agpe**) five, ________ (**rexicese**) one. Are you ________ (**deary**)? Read the ________ (**xett**), please, – er – Sarah Dixon. Sarah? ________ (**hewer**) is Sarah?

Sarah: I'm here. ________ (**rorsy**) I'm ________ (**teal**).

Mr Gray: OK, Sarah. Sit ________ (**wond**) and be ________ (**tique**), please.

(...)

Robert: Can I ________ (**nope**) the ________ (**dwinow**), please?

Mr Gray: OK, but what's that on your ________ (**sked**)? Is it a ________ (**cimoc**)?

Robert: No, it isn't. It's a Maths ________ (**zigamane**).

Mr Gray: Oh, OK. Where are we ________ (**won**)? Oh, yes. Exercise two.

David: This isn't ________ (**yesa**), Mr Gray. What's the ________ (**rensaw**)?

Mr Gray: It's on the ________ (**clabbokard**) with your ________ (**kowhomer**). OK, that's it. ________ (**gribn**) your ________ (**doflers**) here, please.

Robert: ________ (**yeb**), Mr Gray.

Mr Gray: ________ (**egobody**). ________ (**ese**) you ________ (**wormorot**).

2 Say it in English: In class (PB p. 21 / ex. 2)

1. Kannst du „pencil case" buchstabieren?

2. Wo ist meine rote Mappe?

3. Was heißt „Tafel" auf Englisch? – Es heißt …

4. Das ist eine doofe Übung.

5. Mach die Augen zu!

6. Können wir ein Lied singen?

7. Bist du dran? – Tut mir leid, keine Ahnung.

3 Word power: Make pairs (PB p. 21 / ex. 3)

~~cat~~ girls this boys German here pencil terrible ~~dog~~ rubber stand up long short book there magazine on chair sit down brilliant desk English that in

cat – dog		

8 Let's check

Die Lösungen findest du auf S. 96. Aber erst die Übungen bearbeiten, bevor du nachschaust!

1 *Who, what, where* and *how*

1. "__________ are you?" – "I'm Robert Croft."
2. "__________ are you from?" – "I'm from London."
3. "__________'s in your tutor group?" – "Becky, Sarah and David."
4. "__________'s that on your desk?" – "A football magazine."
5. "__________ are Robert and David?" – "They're in the playground."
6. "__________ old are you?" – "I'm twelve."

2 What's in the pictures?

1

2

1. In picture one there are ______________________________

______________________________, but there is only one ______________________________.

2. ______________________________

____

____

3 Which sound?

Say the words and put in the right numbers.

[ɒ] = 1 | [u:] = 2 | [ʌ] = 3 | [ju:] = 4

tutor		**o**range		c**o**lour		t**ou**ch	
sch**oo**l		tr**ue**		gr**ou**p		y**ou**ng	
n**ew**		L**o**ndon		**you**		m**o**nster	

4 Mixed bag

Put in the words: you're your it's (2x) its we're where (3x) they're their there

1. "__________'s __________ picture, Sarah?" – "Look, __________ here." – "Oh, __________ great. I like __________ colours." – "Thank you, David. __________ really nice."
2. "__________ are you from, Becky and Sarah?" – "__________ from Nottingham."
3. "David and Robert are over __________. But __________ are __________ friends?" – "__________ in the playground."

5 Becky and you

Stell dir vor, du bist neu an der Haywood School, und du triffst Becky Burton.

1. Du sagst deinen Namen und, dass du hier neu bist.

____

Hi! Where are you from?

2. Du sagst, wo du herkommst.

____

Oh, from Germany. How old are you?

3. Du sagst, wie alt du bist, und fragst sie, ob sie in deiner Klasse ist.

____

Well, I'm in 7MD. Our tutor is Mrs Dane.

6 Say it in English: At school

1. Wo sind wir? – Wir sind auf S.17, Übung 6. ____________________
2. Ihr seid dran. – Nein, sie sind an der Reihe. ____________________
3. Sie kommen zu spät, Herr Cooper. Wo ist Ihre Tasche? ____________________
4. Wo sind Robert und David? – Sie sind in ihrem Klassenzimmer. ____________________

1 focus Focus on families

1 Becky's family (PB p. 24/ex. 1)

This is Becky Burton's family. Put in the missing names.

Now make sentences.

1. Arthur is Jack's brother.
2. Becky ____________________
3. Paul ____________________
4. Lizzy ____________________
5. Simon ____________________
6. Grace ____________________
7. Peggy ____________________
8. Alan ____________________

2 Who are they? (PB p. 24/ex.1)

1. Your father's mother is your ____________________
2. Your mother's father is your ____________________
3. Your cousin's mother is your ____________________
4. Your mother's brother is your ____________________
5. Your cousin's father is your ____________________
6. Your father's sister is your ____________________

3 Find the words (PB p. 24/ex. 2)

ezuplz ____________________

nosrep ____________________

lpcea ____________________

eatbl ____________________

grthi ____________________

idybrhta ____________________

4 Sounds and spelling (PB p. 25 / ex. 3)

Put these words in the right lists.

my uncle's birthday | Mrs Jones's dog | Mr Smith's house | Liz's computer | her cousin's cat | Pat's pencil | Anuja's name | Jack's friend | Grace's book

[s]	[z]	[ɪz]
___	___	___
___	___	___
___	___	___

5 Anuja's family (PB p. 25 / ex. 4)

Read the text on page 25 of your book. Close the book and put in the missing words.

Anuja's father is ________ and ________. ________ name is Rajiv and ________ from ________. Anuja's mother is ________. ________ tall and ________. Anuja's ________ Anil is ten and ________ ________. Anuja's ________ Balujee is ________. He's ________ to an ________ ________. Her ________ ____ Rosa. Their ________ are ________ nice. Anuja's family is a very ________ family.

6 About your family (PB p. 25 / ex. 6)

a) Draw a picture and write about your family.

This is my family.

____

____

____

____

____

____

____

____

____

b) Now shut your workbook and talk about your family in class.

unit 1 intro

The Burtons and the Dixons

1 Families and houses (PB p. 26 / ex. 1)

These are Robert's photos for his friends in London.

a) Put in the words.

This is the Penrose ____________ – David with his ____________ and ____________, and his ____________ Mark. The girl on the left is his ____________ Jenny from ____________. Their ____________ is in Arndale ____________, in Sherwood.

This is Sarah ____________ house. It's in ____________, but it isn't in the ____________. It's in ____________, too, in ____________ Grove. Sarah is ____________. Her ____________ name is ____________. ____________ is ________ cat.

b) Write about Becky's house and her family.

This is the Burton family – ______________________________

____

____

____

Becky's house ______________________________

____

______________________________.

2 *s'* or *'s*? (PB p. 27 / ex. 2)

Crofts | girls | ~~Becky~~ | Dixons | cousins | Jones | Mrs Dane | Burtons | Sarah | David

1. Barker is Becky's dog. 2. David is in ____________ tutor group. 3. The ____________ pictures are very funny. 4. The ____________ bike shop is in Mansfield Road. 5. *Anuja*: My ____________ names are Tejinder and Rita. 6. The ____________ and the ____________ houses are in Larwood Grove. 7. Tabby is ____________ cat. 8. Grandma ____________ ideas are brilliant. 9. Jenny is ____________ cousin from Germany.

3 Word power: A puzzle (PB p. 27 / ex. 3)

1. The Burtons' ▒ is in Sherwood.
2. There's a window in the ▒.
3. It's in your pencil case.
4. Four walls, a door and windows? What is it? A ▒.
5. A big shop:
6. In the Burtons' shop you can see new ▒.
7. A green place with trees next to a house. What is it? A ▒.
8. You can put your car in the ▒.
9. A word pair: right – ▒.
10. Mr Burton is in the bike ▒.
11. Let's go in! Open the ▒!
12. It's on the house: ▒
13. English for "Flur": ▒

Down: A place in Sherwood ▒.

4 Word power: What's inside and outside the house? (PB p. 27 / ex. 3)

Find the words.

B	E	E	D	S	R	F	G	H	O	K	E
A	K	L	U	T	Z	E	Q	W	A	L	L
T	D	G	A	R	L	E	N	U	J	K	O
H	G	F	K	I	T	C	H	E	N	A	S
R	A	G	H	A	L	L	U	Z	G	A	A
O	R	O	O	H	G	F	E	S	C	H	T
O	D	H	U	O	Z	T	H	S	W	U	O
M	E	G	A	R	A	G	E	H	I	K	L
I	N	H	U	R	P	P	O	O	N	E	E
L	G	V	S	O	C	G	E	V	D	P	O
B	E	D	R	O	O	M	E	N	O	L	L
E	O	O	C	F	T	R	E	E	W	E	S

→

1. Bedroom
2. Hall
3. Garden ↓
4. Garage
5.
6.

↓

7. Bath
8.
9.
10.

1 What have they got? (PB p. 28 / ex. 1)

Write the sentences. Use long forms

1. Becky has got a stereo.
2. ______________________
3. ______________________
4. ______________________
5. ______________________
6. ______________________

2 Questions and answers (PB p. 29 / ex. 3)

Use the right forms of ***have got.***

1. ________ Becky ________ a football poster? – No, she ________. She ________ animal posters.
2. ________ Simon ________ a skateboard? – Yes, he ________, but he ________ a computer.
3. ________ the Burtons ________ CDs in their shop? – No, they ________. They ________ bikes.
4. ________ Simon ________ comics in his school bag? – No, he ________. He ________ a German book in his school bag.
5. ________ David ________ a brother? – Yes, he ________, and he ________ a German cousin.
6. ________ Becky and Sarah ________ a nice English teacher? – Yes, they ________, and they ________ a nice German teacher, too.
7. ________ the Dixons ________ a boy? – No, they ________. They ________ two girls.

3 *A* or *an*? (PB p. 29 / ex. 4)

Make two lists in your exercise book, one for ***a*** and one for ***an***. Put these words in the right lists.

teacher, unit, Indian, game, Italian, room, CD, idea, stereo, nose, alphabet, answer, word, horse, animal, pencil, eye, racket, example, window, class, exercise

4 *Can/can't* (PB p. 29)

Can you make sentences?

1. football • play • in • can • we • park • the — We can play football in the park.
2. folder • I • green • find • can't • my ____________________.
3. listen • to • new • CD • we • can • the ____________________.
4. you • spell • 'animal' • can ____________________?
5. go • we • swimming pool • to • the • can't ____________________?
6. I • you • ask • question • can • a ____________________?
7. open • we • window • can • the ____________________?
8. you • in • come • can't ____________________.

5 School (PB p. 29)

Find the right sentences.

1. I must do my English homework.
2. ____________________
3. ____________________
4. ____________________
5. ____________________

____

Breakfast at the Dixons' house!

language B

1 True or false? (PB p. 30/ex. 1)

Are these sentences true or false?
Correct the false sentences in your exercise book.

	true	false
1. It's Friday morning at the Crofts' house.	☐	☐
2. Sarah and her family are in the living room.	☐	☐
3. It's Sarah's turn to set the table.	☐	☐
4. Kim hasn't got a knife.	☐	☐
5. Mrs Dixon has got the knives.	☐	☐
6. Kim's lunchbox is in Sarah's bag.	☐	☐
7. Kim's got a new bike.	☐	☐
8. Becky's parents haven't got locks and pumps in their shop.	☐	☐
9. Sarah and Kim aren't always good friends.	☐	☐

2 What they *have* or *haven't got* (PB p. 30 / ex. 1)

Ask and answer five questions in your exercise book.
Example: Has Becky got a bike? No, she hasn't.

✗ = no ✔ = yes

	new Underdogs CD	bike	skateboard	computer
Becky	✔	✗	✗	✔
Simon	✗	✔	✔	✗
David	✔	✗	✔	✔
Sarah	✗	✔	✗	✗
Robert	✗	✔	✗	✗

3 Play a game: Snakes and Ladders (Ausschneidebögen 2+3; PB p. 31 / ex. 4)

4 Sounds and spelling (PB p. 30 / ex. 2)

You say:	You write:	You say:	You write:	You say:	You write:
1. [naɪf]	________	4. [spu:n]	________	7. ['sɔ:sə]	________
2. ['lʌntʃbɒks]	________	5. [kʌp]	________	8. ['bɒtl]	________
3. [pleɪt]	________	6. [bəʊl]	________	9. [pʌmp]	________

5 Write sentences (PB p. 31 / ex. 5)

Make sentences like 1. a) and 1. b). Use the words in the box.

brilliant CD • funny comics • fast skates • ~~lazy sister~~ •
two English cousins • nice teacher • blue bowl • great garden

1. a) Sarah has got a lazy sister. b) Sarah's sister is lazy.
2. a) Robert ________ b) ________
3. a) The Burtons ________ b) ________
4. a) The girls ________ b) ________
5. a) The children ________ b) ________
6. a) Barker ________ b) ________
7. a) David ________ b) ________
8. a) Jenny ________ b) ________

The frog (I)

1 Find the right sentence (PB p. 33 / ex. 2)

1. *Simon*: Let's take the frog home.

Robert: ______________________
Simon: We can play a trick on Becky!

A That's not a good idea.
B Yes, that's a great idea.
C Home? Why?

2. *Becky*: Let's listen to a CD.

Sarah: ______________________

____
Becky: Yes, why not.

A We haven't got a CD player.
B I must go to the supermarket.
C Good idea. What about your new Underdogs CD?

3. *Sarah*: Aaah! Becky!

Becky: ______________________
Sarah: It's under the desk now!

A It's a nice frog. Come here, little frog.
B Er … Sarah.
C It's Sunday afternoon.

4. *Becky*: It's OK, little frog. I'm your friend.

Sarah: ______________________

____
Becky: Mmm. Good question.

A Good idea. I like frogs.
B That's funny. How can a frog get into your room?
C Where's Barker? Can't he play with the little frog?

5. *Becky*: What about the plates, Simon?

Simon: ______________________
Mrs B: Becky, can you call Dad? Tea's ready.

A I need a new lock for my bike.
B Oh, yes. They're in the cupboard.
C It's teatime.

6. *Simon*: Aaah! Mum! Mum!

Mrs B: ______________________

____
Simon: A frog! In the cupboard! Look!

A Don't be silly, Simon!
B Tea's ready.
C What's the matter, Simon? Are you OK?

2 What's that in English? (PB p. 33 / ex. 3)

1. What's "Ich habe eine Idee" in English?

____

2. What about "Was ist los"?

____

3. What's "Meine Lieblingstiere sind Frösche"?

____

____

4. What's "Kann ich hereinkommen"?

____

5. And what's "Das habe ich schon"?

____

6. What about "Du musst dir diese CD anhören"?

____

____

1 *Have they* or *haven't they?* (PB p. 34 / ex. 1)

Make questions and answers. Use ***have got, has got, haven't got*** and ***hasn't got.***

Example: 1. The Dixons: a dog ✗, a cat ✔

Have the Dixons got a dog? – No, they haven't. They've got a cat.

2. David: sister ✗, brother ✔

____

3. The Burtons: swimming pool ✗, garden ✔

____

____

4. Sarah: horse ✗, cat ✔

____

5. Robert: a CD player ✔

____

6. Becky: computer ✔

____

2 What's right: *a* or *an?* (PB p. 34 / ex. 2)

1. _an_ exercise book	_a_ new exercise book	6. ___ question	___ easy question
2. ___ page	___ empty page	7. ___ example	___ good example
3. ___ exercise	___ funny exercise	8. ___ German school	___ English school
4. ___ answer	___ silly answer	9. ___ idea	___ good idea
5. ___ book	___ Italian book	10. ___ girl	___ Indian girl

3 Find the words (PB p. 35 / ex. 4)

tt (3x) **oo** (6x) **ll** (5x) **nn** (2x) **ss** (1x) **mm** (1x) **ee** (2x) **dd** (1x)

1. r___f	6. ma___er	11. d___r	16. E___y
2. te___is	7. li___le	12. bedr___m	17. bri___iant
3. bo___le	8. swi___ing p___l	13. gla___	18. fu___y
4. aftern___n	9. tr___	14. ca___	19. si___y
5. sp___n	10. ha___	15. n___d	20. Arnot Hi___ Park

52
4 Sounds and spelling (PB p. 35 / ex. 6)

Listen and put the words in the right lists.

a)

[f]	[v]

53 b)

[z]	[s]

Tipp
Lege deine Hände über die Ohren. Sage [z] oder [v], danach sage [s] or [f]. Wenn du [z] oder [v] sagst, kannst du ein Summen hören, wenn du aber [s] oder [f] sagst, hörst du keins.

5 What *can* they do? What *can't* they do? (PB p.35 / ex. 7)

1. David can say "Guten Tag" in German.
2. Becky ______
3. Robert ______
4. Mark ______
5. David ______
6. Barker ______

6 Sorry, I can't (PB p.35 / ex. 7)

Make questions and answers.

Can you	go to the park play football go to the swimming pool ...	with me?	**Sorry, I can't.** • **I must**	do my homework. go to the supermarket. go and see my grandma. ...

revision 1
Let's start – Unit 1

Deine Lösungen zu *Revision* kannst du auf S. 96 immer selbst überprüfen.

1 Questions and answers

Make questions and answers. Use ***have got/haven't got, has got/hasn't got, are/aren't, can/can't.***
Example: Barker: play tennis ✗, play football ✓
Can Barker play tennis? – No, he can't, but he can play football.

1. Kim: Sarah's CD ✗, lunchbox ✓
2. Robert: draw a horse ✗, draw a cat ✓
3. The Burtons: supermarket ✗, bike shop ✓
4. The children: in the classroom ✗, in the playground ✓
5. Becky: football posters in her room ✗, animal posters ✓

1. ____________________

2 What's in the pictures?

Make sentences with ***there is/there are*** and ***this/that.*** Write in your exercise book.

Example:
← There is one boy in this picture, but there are
↓ three boys in that picture.

3 Sounds and spelling

Put the words in the right lists and find more examples.

Burtons • but • computer • full • hurt • must • spoon • under • put • turn • foot • tutor

[ʌ]	[ʊ]	[u:]	[ɜ:]

4 *This / that, these / those*

Put in the right words.

1. ____________ dog here is nice, but ____________ dog isn't.
2. ____________ houses over there are very old.
3. ____________ trees here are small, but ____________ over there are very big.
4. ____________ skateboard is fast, but ____________ skateboard isn't.
5. The children are in ____________ pictures, and their parents are in ____________ pictures over there.
6. ____________ is Sarah's picture and ____________ is Simon's picture.
7. ____________ bikes here are new, and ____________ bikes over there are old.
8. Are ____________ pencils over there from your pencil case, Robert?
9. ____________ is my mum and ____________ is my dad.
10. Are ____________ your football magazines here, Simon?

5 Word power: These words go together

1. knives, forks, spoons ____________
2. read, write, ____________
3. bike, pump, ____________
4. bowl, plate, ____________
5. men, women, ____________
6. dog, cat, ____________
7. lunch, tea, ____________
8. bed, table, ____________
9. leg, foot, ____________
10. bike, skates, ____________
11. English, German, ____________

6 Say it in English: Say no

1. Bin ich dran? – Nein, die Mädchen sind dran. ____________

____

2. Lass uns zusammen gehen! – Nein, geh du alleine. ____________

____

3. Kann ich reinkommen? – Nein, tut mir Leid. Ich habe zu tun. ____________

____

In town

1 What you can see in town (PB p. 38 / ex. 2)

Look at the pictures and find the words in the puzzle.

2 I'm new in town (PB p. 39 / ex. 3)

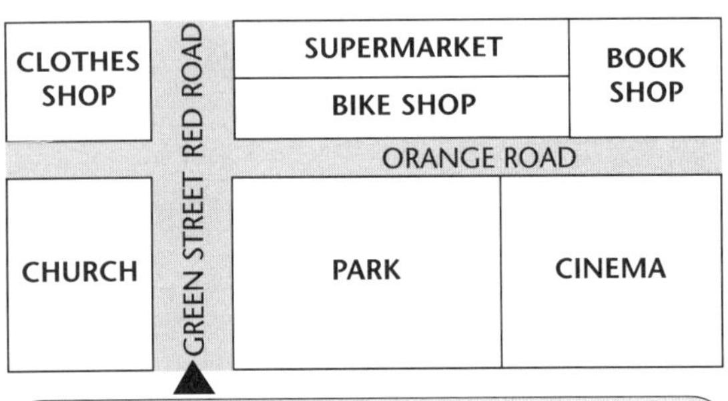

Look at the map and put in the missing words.

______________. Can you ______________ the ______________ the bookshop?

Yes, of course. Go ______________ and ______________ into ______________. ______________ and the bookshop is ______________.

______________. Where can ______________ a supermarket, please?

Oh, ______________ a supermarket not ______________ here. ______________ into ______________. The supermarket is ______________, next to the bike shop.

54 3 Find the way (PB p. 39 / ex. 3)

a) Listen to the two dialogues and find the ways. Draw the man's way in red and the girl's way in blue.

Where are they going?

Man: ____________________

Girl: ____________________

b) Work with a partner. Make new dialogues.

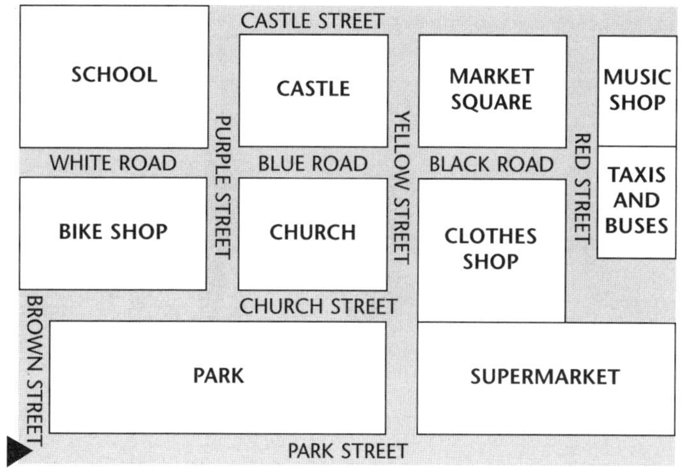

Shopping

language **A**

1 A busy day in town (PB p. 40 / ex. 1)

play | ~~buy~~ | watch | play with | fight | listen | look at | laugh at | sing

What are the people doing? Write ten sentences.

1. A woman is buying ____________________
2. ____________________
3. ____________________
4. ____________________
5. ____________________
6. ____________________
7. ____________________
8. ____________________
9. ____________________
10. ____________________

2 Is it true? (PB p. 40 / ex. 2)

This Friday afternoon the Dixons are in the living room. Make questions and answers.

1. Sarah and Kim • fight?

Are Sarah and Kim fighting? – No, they aren't. They're watching TV.

2. Sarah and Kim • laugh?

___

3. The cat • watch TV?

___

4. Mr Dixon • write e-mails?

___

5. Mrs Dixon • open door?

___

6. It • rain[1]?

___

[1] to rain – [reɪn] regnen

3 Word power (PB p. 41 / ex. 4)

Put in the missing words.

1. Come on! Let's go to the shops now. — _ _ _ _ _ a _ _ _ _ _ _ _ ! I can't find my bag.
2. You can't come into the shop with skates. — That's OK. I can _ _ _ _ outside.
3. Have you got the cinema tickets? — Yes. They're in my _ _ _.
4. OK, here's your _ _ _ _ _ _ _ _ _ _ _, Anil. — Great! Thanks, Mum. Now I can _ _ _ the new Underdogs CD.
5. Oh! We can't go outside. — Let's watch the 'Tom and Jerry' _ _ _ _ _ _ _ _ _ on _ _.
6. Can't we listen to a _ _ _ _ _ _ _ _ _ _ _ CD? This music is terrible! — OK, I've got a great Madonna CD.

Can you fetch us, Mum?

1 The *'ing'* form (PB p. 42 / ex. 2)

Make *'ing'* forms and put them in the right lists.

~~come~~ ~~buy~~ ~~sit~~ stop go phone put clap spend write get take carry wait make

+ ing	~~e~~ + ing	+ (Doppelkonsonant) + ing
buying,	coming,	sitting,

2 What can you see in the pictures? (PB p. 42 / ex. 2)

write ~~get~~ phone stop look read ~~sit~~ (2x) ~~rain~~ come watch go

The two girls aren't sitting on the chairs. They are sitting on the table.

It's raining, but the boy and the girl aren't getting wet.

3 Who has got my new video? (PB p. 43 / ex. 4)

Sarah is phoning her friends. Put in: me you (2x) him her it (3x) us (2x) them

1. *Sarah*: Hi, David. I can't find my new video. Maybe Jenny has got ______. Can I talk to ______?
David: Er … Mark's here, but I can't see Jenny. She isn't with ______. Maybe she's with Becky and Simon. You can phone ______.

2. *Sarah*: Hello, Becky. Is Jenny with ______?
Becky: No, she isn't with ______.
Sarah: Have you got my new video?
Becky: No, I haven't. Maybe Robert has got ______.
Sarah: OK, I can phone ______.

3. *Sarah*: Hi, Robert. Is Jenny with ______? I can't find my new video, and maybe she's got ______.
Robert: Yes, she's with ______. We're watching your video. It's brilliant.

4 Mixed bag (PB p. 43 / ex. 6)

Look at the pictures. What are the different people doing and what are they saying?
Put in the missing words.

1. A boy ______ to ______ sister.
Sister: Sorry, I can't ______ . I ______ ______ to my new CD.

2. Two boys ______ in a tree. They ______ at ______ sister.
Boys: Ha, ha! She can't ______ !

3. A girl ______ with ______ dog.
Girl: Good boy. Go and ______ .

4. A woman ______ a man the way to the shopping centre. *Woman:* Excuse ______. Can you ______ ______ the way to the shopping centre?

text

The race

1 True or false? (PB p. 44–45 / ex. 1)

a) Read the text again. Are these sentences true or false?

True	False	
☐	☐	1. It is raining, and David, Jenny, Sarah and Robert are getting off the bus in Sherwood.
☐	☐	2. Jenny has got the tickets in her bag.
☐	☐	3. This Sunday afternoon Martins Media is very busy.
☐	☐	4. Lots of people are watching a cartoon on a big TV.
☐	☐	5. In the race, Sarah and Robert can go by bus, and David and Jenny must walk.
☐	☐	6. Sarah and Robert's bus is the number twelve.
☐	☐	7. The bus is stopping in front of the castle, and David and Jenny can see Robert and Sarah.
☐	☐	8. Ten minutes later, three people are running towards the statue.

b) Correct the false sentences. Write in your exercise book.

2 Who is saying what? (PB p. 44–45 / ex. 1)

Make correct sentences and write down who is saying what in the story.

a) a minute ...	e) the champions, my friend ...	i) you are, young man. ✔
b) a long time for a bus today!	f) from here to the Robin Hood statue.	j) get off here.
c) see them.	g) you two.	k) far?
d) a bus?	h) Day Rider Tickets.	

1. Driver ____: Four Day Rider tickets. Here you are, young man.
2. ____: Let's ____
3. ____: Is it ____
4. ____: We've got ____
5. ____: Let's have a race – ____
6. ____: You can wait ____
7. ____: We are ____
8. ____: Er, wait ____
9. ____: I can't ____
10. ____: Hi, ____
11. ____: Why aren't you on ____

3 Find more words
(PB p. 46 / ex. 3)

1 Where are they and what are they doing? (PB p. 47 / ex. 1)

Look at the example and make sentences.

1. Robert • shop • not look • CDs • buy • book — Robert is in a shop. He isn't looking at CDs. He's buying a book.
2. Simon • garden • not play • ball • play • Barker ______________________________
3. Sarah and Kim • living room • not watch • TV • watch • video ______________________________
4. Becky • room • not read • comics • write • e-mail ______________________________
5. Mr and Mrs Burton • home • not work • listen • music ______________________________
6. Jenny • outside • not walk • shops • wait • bus ______________________________

2 Word power (PB p. 47 / ex. 1)

Find the words and match them to the right pictures.

1. t e w — w e t [a]
2. t e l e t r — _ _ _ _ _ _ [ ]
3. v e r d i r — _ _ _ _ _ _ [ ]
4. b o l e i m — _ _ _ _ _ _ [ ]
5. n w i — _ _ _ [ ]
6. f o b e d y n i r — _ _ _ _ _ _ _ _ _ [ ]
7. t a s l — _ _ _ _ [ ]

a

b
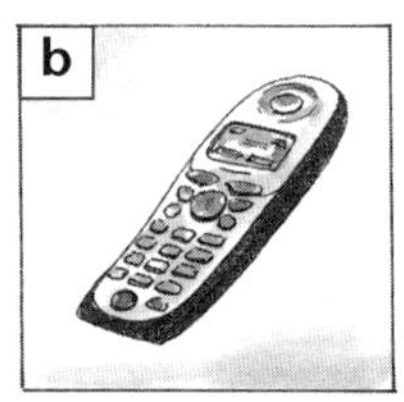
c

d

e

f

g

3 What's missing? (PB p. 47 / ex. 2)

Put in the missing words and finish the dialogue.

Jim and Linda are in town. ______________ have got a lot of shopping.

Jim: Oh no, ______________'s raining, and look at all these shopping bags! ______________ can't carry ______________ all. Let's phone Mum and ask ______________ to fetch ______________.

Linda: Good idea! Have ______________ got ______________ mobile with ______________ ?

Jim: Sorry, ______________ 's at home.

Linda: Great! ______________ phone is at home, too. Look, there's Mike. Maybe ______________ 's got ______________ mobile with ______________ .

Jim: Hey, Mike! Mike, wait! Oh no, ______________ can't hear ______________ . Mike! Mike!

4 What can you say? (PB p. 47 / ex. 3)

What can you say to your friend? Finish the short dialogues.

Your friend:	You:
1. Oh, this is your bag. Here you are.	______________
2. Don't lose those tickets!	______________
3. Is the new shop far from here?	______________
4. Which is our bus?	______________
5. It's starting to rain.	______________
6. I'm ready now.	______________
7. Look! There's a big shopping centre.	______________
8. Can I talk to your brother, please?	______________
9. Oops! Sorry! Are you hurt?	______________
10. See you tomorrow!	______________

Tipp

Du hast jetzt so viel Englisch gelernt, dass du die richtigen Redemittel parat hast, um auf bestimmte englische Äußerungen angemessen zu reagieren. Momentan hast du allerdings noch nicht so viel Gelegenheit, in echte englischsprachige Situationen zu kommen. Bei Übungen wie dieser ist es daher ganz wichtig, dass du dich in eine echte Situation hineindenkst, in der diese Sätze gesprochen werden könnten.

focus

2 Focus on numbers

1 Numbers 1–12 (p. 48 / ex. 1)

a) Write the numbers in words.

1. two + one = three

2. ______________ ______________

3. ______________ ______________

4. ______________ ______________

5. ______________ ______________

6. ______________ ______________

7. ______________ ______________

8. ______________ ______________

9. ______________ ______________

10. ______________ ______________

b) What are the two missing numbers? ______________ and ______________.

2 More numbers (p. 48 / ex. 2)

Write the numbers.

[ ][ ] fifteen

[ ][ ] nineteen

[ ][ ] twenty-four

[ ][ ] sixty-eight

[ ][ ][ ] one hundred and forty-four

[ ][ ][ ] seven hundred and thirty-nine

[ ],[ ][ ][ ] one thousand and one

[ ],[ ][ ][ ] five thousand and fifty-eight

[ ],[ ][ ][ ] nine thousand, four hundred and fifty-three

[ ],[ ][ ][ ],[ ][ ][ ]
one million, two hundred and thirty thousand, two hundred and sixty-four

56 3 Robert's new home (p. 48 / ex. 4)

a) Listen to Robert and put in the right numbers.

1. People in London: ______________
2. People in Nottingham: ______________
3. Parks in Nottingham: ______________
4. Cinemas in Nottingham: ______________
5. Markets in Nottingham: ______________
6. Shops in Victoria Shopping Centre: ______________

b) Now write the numbers in words.

1. ______________________________________

____

____

4 What are they buying? (p. 49 / ex. 5)

The Penroses are at the shopping centre. Look at the pictures and say what they are all buying.
Write the sentences in your exercise book. Example: Mrs Penrose is buying a ... for thirty-five pounds ...

5 Different clothes (p.49 / ex. 6)

a) Put in the missing words.

b) Who is who? Write sentences in your exercise book about Mark, Simon, Mrs Dixon, Mrs Croft and Mr Penrose.

Example:
The boy with the sweatshirt and ... is Mark.

6 Your shop (p. 49 / ex. 7)

a) Colour in the different clothes in your shop. Put in how much they are. Look at the example: £2.99

b) Now work with a partner. Partner A is a customer at partner B's shop. Then partner B is a customer at partner A's shop. Make short dialogues. You can use the words on the right.

Can I help you?

Have you got ... ?

Sorry, we haven't got ...

What about ... ?

I like ... We've got ...

I need ... ... very good.

How much ... ?

Yes, ... fine, thank you.

Free time

1 In the park (PB p. 50/ex. 1)

It is Friday evening. Look at the picture and say what the different people are doing in the park. Write your sentences in your exercise book. Start like this: *A man is watching the tennis players.*

2 What day is it? (PB p. 51/ex. 4)

1. It is the day after Wednesday: ____________________
2. These are the days of the weekend: ____________________ and ____________________
3. The day with seven letters in it: ____________________
4. The last day of school in the week: ____________________
5. It's school again! ____________________

3 What time is it now? (PB p. 51/ex. 5)

57

a) Listen to the dialogues. Say what time it is.

1. ____________ 2. ____________ 3. ____________ 4. ____________

b) Listen again and say what the different children are doing.

1. ____________________
2. ____________________
3. ____________________
4. ____________________

4 Draw the right times (Ausschneidebogen 4; PB p. 51 / ex. 5)

 twenty-three minutes past six	 eleven ten	 twelve minutes to four	 five forty-eight	 ten to three	 nine fifty-three

Use your clock and ask your partner the time.

Jenny's day

language **A**

1 Jenny's day (PB p. 52/ex. 1b)

Which sentences from the text ***Jenny's day*** go with the pictures?

Start like this: I never get up before eight o'clock ...

2 Mrs Dane's favourite day (PB p. 53 / ex. 4)

Find the verbs and put them in the right places. Cross out the adverbs in the wrong places.

vahe ______________	My favourite day is Saturday. I ***always*** get up at nine o'clock ~~***always***~~
eltins ______________	and ______________ a nice bath. I ***sometimes*** ______________
teg ______________	***sometimes*** to a nice CD, and I ***often*** ______________ a book ***often*** in the
ahev ______________	bath. At ten o'clock I ***usually*** ______________ ***usually*** breakfast in the
og ______________	kitchen. ***Never*** I ***never*** ______________ to the shops before half past
chatw ______________	eleven. In the afternoon I ***sometimes*** am ***sometimes*** outside and
dear ______________	______________ in the garden or I ______________ TV. In the evening
etem ______________	I ***usually*** ______________ my friends ***usually***. Saturdays ***always*** are
krow ______________	***always*** great: there is no school!

3 A sunny Saturday afternoon (PB p. 53 / ex. 7)

This Saturday afternoon it is very sunny, so these people are doing different things today.
Look at the pictures and say what they usually do on Saturdays and what they are doing this Saturday.
Write the sentences in your exercise book.

Example: The Burtons usually go out in their car on Saturdays, but today they ...

1 The Burtons

2 Robert and David

3 Mr and Mrs Penrose

4 Kim and Sarah

5 Mr and Mrs Singh

6 Anuja and Anil

1 Word power (PB p. 54 / ex. 1)

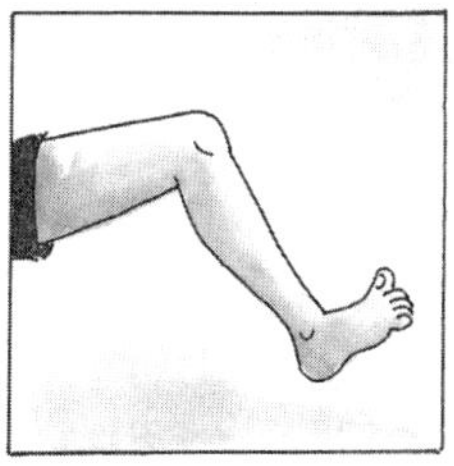

________ ________ ________ to ________ to ________

________ ________ ________ to ________ to ________

2 "Stupid dog!" (PB p. 54 / ex. 1)

Put in the right verbs in their right forms. shout ~~show~~ do go fly chase wave hit come

Robert shows ________ his new scooter to David. Robert's scooter ________ really fast. Robert ________ tricks on his scooter. He ________ with his free hand and leg. A dog ________ a rabbit in front of Robert. Robert's scooter ________ something and he ________ into a big bush. When Robert ________ out of the bush, he ________, "Stupid dog!"

3 Sounds and spelling (PB p. 54 / ex. 2)

Put these verbs into the third person singular.
Then put them in the right lists.
Can you find more examples?

~~hit~~ • ~~play~~ • ~~rush~~ • shout • finish • go • turn • watch • start • carry • wave • fly • fetch • come • say • pick up • get • chase • cry • match

[z]	[s]	[ɪz]
plays,	hits,	rushes,

4 Write about your partner (PB p. 55 / ex. 3)

a) Work with a partner. Exchange workbooks with your partner and write your name in the box.
Now put a ✓ to say how often you do the things in the list.

Name: ________	always	usually	often	sometimes	never
help your mum and dad					
ride a scooter					
watch videos					
get angry					
go to the theatre					
carry the shopping					
buy CDs					

b) Now look at your own workbook again. Use the list to write about your partner in your exercise book.
Example: My partner Michael often helps his mum and dad. He never …

c) Make little dialogues with your partner:
Example: I always get up at 6 o'clock. What about you? – I usually get up at …

5 Late for school! (PB p. 55 / ex. 5)

Jenny and David are late for school this morning. Put in the right times and the missing words.
Put the verbs in the right forms.

sleep
get up
7.30 am

It's two minutes past __________. David is __________. He usually __________ at __________.

be
bathroom
have breakfast
this time

It's __________. Jenny __________ in the __________. She usually __________ at __________.

walk
school
this morning
go

It's __________. David and Jenny usually __________ to __________. But __________ __________ they __________ by bike.

come
playground
be
in Assembly

It's __________. David and Jenny __________ into the __________. They __________ usually __________ at this time.

have lunch
their friends
work
classroom

It's __________. They usually __________ with __________. But now they __________ in the __________.

Barker's story

1 What happens? (PB p. 56–57 / ex. 1)

Read ***Barker's story*** again and say what happens …

1. At 7.30 in the morning he ____________________
2. At 8.20 ____________________
3. On Saturdays ____________________
4. When Tabby comes into the garden, ____________________
5. Every Sunday ____________________
6. When the Burtons go out for picnics, ____________________
7. In the evening ____________________
8. At 9 o'clock in the evening ____________________

2 A good text (PB p. 5 / ex. 2)

Read the short text. Now make it better.
Write it again and use the words under the text to connect the sentences.

My name is Barker. I often bark. I bark at dogs in cars. They bark at me. I bark at cats, too. I don't like them. Sometimes the neighbour's cat comes into our garden. I bark at her. She always runs away. I chase her. I'm dog-tired.

and | and then

then | after that | because

____

____

____

____

____

____

____

____

Tipp

Wenn du längere Texte schreibst, kannst du die Wörter ***and, and then*** und ***because*** verwenden, um zwei Sätze zu verbinden und einen daraus zu machen.
Du kannst die Wörter ***then*** und ***after that*** benutzen, um einen neuen Satz anzufangen und ihn mit dem Satz davor zu verknüpfen.

3 The bike race (PB p. 58 / ex. 2)

a) Look at the four pictures. You can use them to write a story.

1

2

3

4

b) Put your ideas in the lists.

Who? Write the children's names	What happens in the story?
	show new bike, laugh at,
	have a race,
Where are they?	
What day and what time is it?	

c) Use your lists to tell the story to the class. Then write the story. Connect your sentences! You can exchange exercise books with your partner and correct his / her story.

1 Word power: Odd word out (PB p. 59 / ex. 1)

a) Which is the odd word out in each list? Underline it.

1. dinner • lunch • breakfast • muesli

2. Monday • weekend • Friday • Tuesday

3. usually • middle • often • sometimes

4. Assembly • pupils • England • subject

______ ______ ______ ______

5. scooter • rabbit • bike • skates

6. love • walk • run • ride

7. theatre • kitchen • church • road

8. hill • pet • tree • park

______ ______ ______ ______

b) Find a fourth word for each list.

2 Hammy the hamster (PB p. 59 / ex. 2)

Put in the right forms of the verbs.

shout (2x) • do • look • ride • be (4x) • go (2x) • look after • live • play • hate • stand up • come • love • sit

Hello, I ______ Hammy the hamster. I ______ in Rajiv's room. Sometimes it ______ very boring: Rajiv ______ his bike to school early every morning, and he ______ home at quarter to four. So I ______ often alone. Rajiv ______ his homework now, so I ______ on his bed. Oh, no! There ______ the neighbour's terrible cats again. They ______ at the window and they ______ at me. Rajiv ______ them, too. He always ______ at them. Yes, he ______ now and he is ______ to the window. " ______ home for dinner, you two", he ______. I ______ Rajiv because he always ______ me.

3 Your favourite animal

a) Write about your pet or your favourite animal in your exercise book. The verbs in the box can help you with ideas.

play • sleep • chase • like • teach • sit • ...

You can start like this: We have got a ... .
... name is ... .

Or you can start like this: We haven't got a pet, but I like ... because ... .

b) Find a picture of your pet or animal, or draw one for your text.
Be ready to talk about this in class.

Your animal

Unit 2 – Unit 3

1 Places in town

Look at the map and read the text. Find the way and write the different places on the map.

Go down Park Road. The castle is on the left. Turn left into Red Row. You can see the park on the right. Turn right into Castle Road. Go down Castle Road into Brown Row. There is a cinema on the right. Turn right into Black Road and right again into Green Street.
There is a shopping centre on the left. Turn left into King Street and you can see a bookshop on the right. Turn right into Church Street. Turn right again into Red Row. The church is on the left. There is a café next to the bookshop.

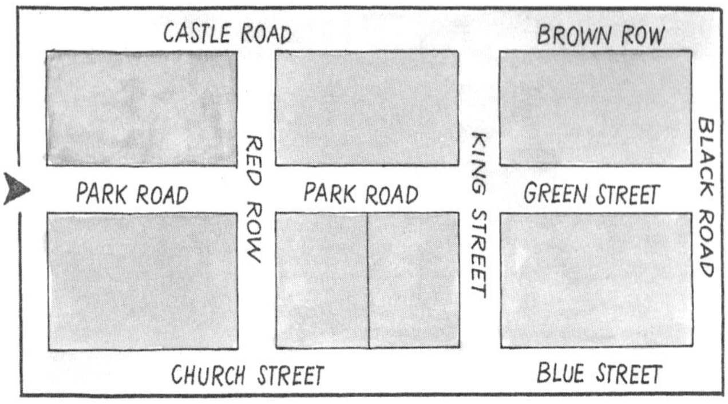

2 Free time in the park

Look at the two pictures and write about them. Write the sentences in your exercise book.

a) It's 2 o'clock in the afternoon.
Example: Two boys are riding their scooters.

b) Now it's 2.15 in the afternoon.
Example: The two boys aren't riding their scooters. They are sitting under a tree.

3 Mixed bag: At the clothes shop

What are David, Jenny and the shop assistant saying? Put in the missing words and finish the dialogue.

Shop assistant: Can ______ help ______?

Jenny: Er … no thanks. ______ 're just looking.

David: Oh look, Jenny! These jeans are only £11. ______ 's a special offer, but ______ can't find the ______ size.

Jenny: Let's ask the assistant. Maybe she ______ help ______.

What's ______ size, David?

David: Oh, 25.

Jenny: Excuse ______. Have ______ got these jeans in size 25?

Shop assistant: Let's see. Yes, here ______ are.

David: Great! – Oh dear!

Jenny: What's the matter?

David: ______'ve only got £8 with ______.

My name is

AB 1

Snakes and Ladders

(für 2 – 4 Spieler)

Ihr braucht Buntstifte, einen Würfel und Spielfiguren für alle Mitspieler.
Malt zunächst das Spielfeld und die Karten an.
Schneidet dann die Karten aus.

Spielregeln:

Mischt die Karten und legt sie verdeckt auf einen Stapel.
Setzt alle Figuren auf das Startfeld. Würfelt darum, wer beginnen darf. Ihr würfelt der Reihe nach und zieht mit eurer Figur entsprechend der Anzahl der gewürfelten Augen los.
Wenn ihr auf ein Kartenfeld *(Pick a card)* kommt, nehmt ihr eine Karte vom Stapel. Dann sagt ihr auf Englisch, was ihr auf der Karte seht, und buchstabiert sowohl die Singular- als auch die Pluralform des Wortes. Je nachdem, wo ihr euch befindet, passiert Folgendes:
Wenn ihr euch am unteren Ende einer Leiter befindet, dürft ihr für eine richtige Antwort nach oben klettern bis ans obere Ende der Leiter. Antwortet ihr falsch, bleibt ihr stehen, wo ihr seid, und der nächste Spieler ist an der Reihe.
Wenn ihr euch am Kopf einer Schlange befindet, rutscht ihr bei einer falschen Antwort nach unten bis ans Schwanzende. Antwortet ihr richtig, bleibt ihr stehen, wo ihr seid, und der nächste Spieler ist an der Reihe.
Wer zuerst ins Ziel *(Finish)* kommt, hat gewonnen.

Tipp: Wenn ihr neue Pluralformen gelernt habt, könnt ihr weitere Karten für das Spiel malen.

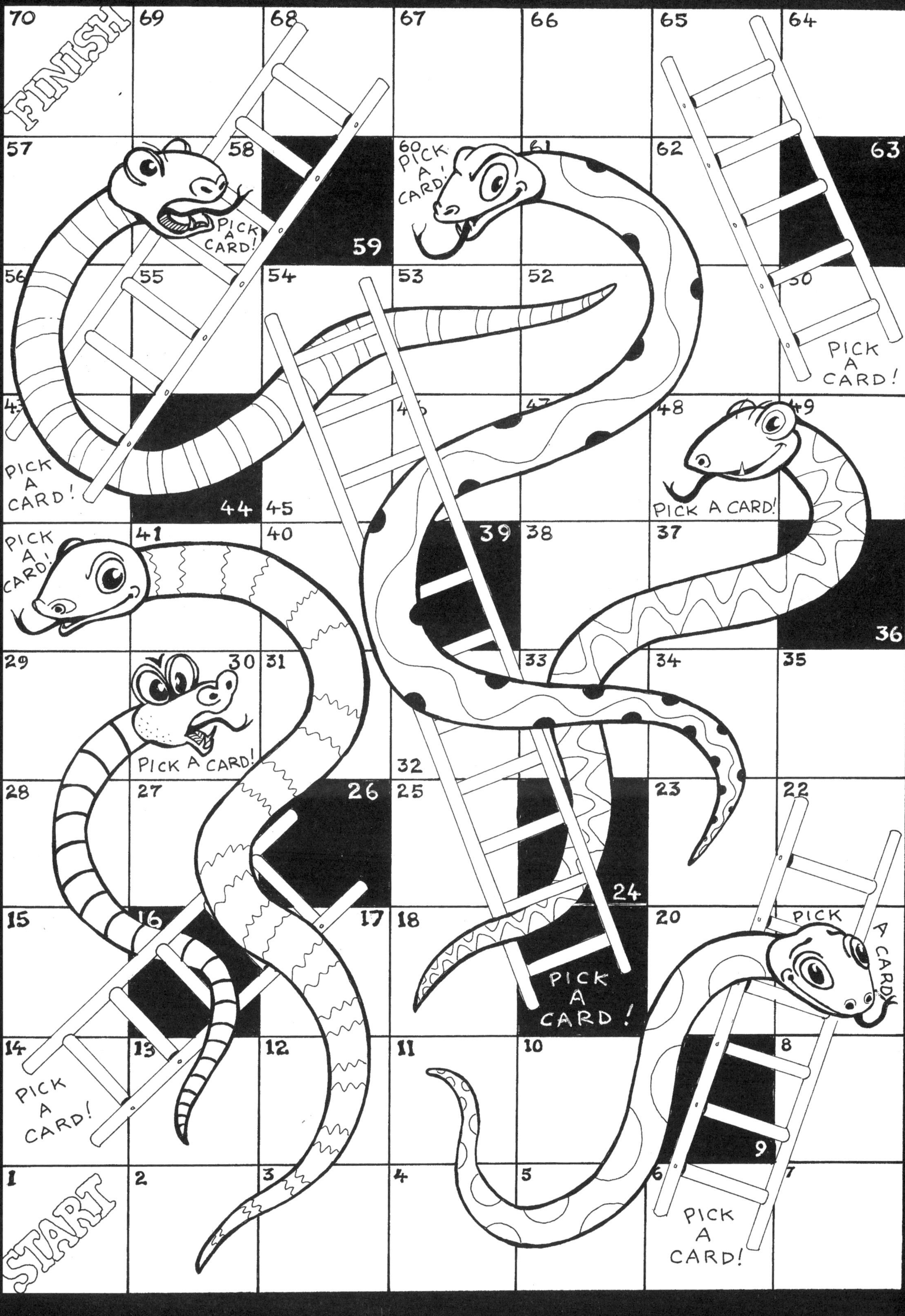
70 FINISH
69
68
67
66
65
64
57
58
PICK A CARD!
60 PICK A CARD!
61
62
63
59
56
55
54
53
52
50
PICK A CARD!
48
49
PICK A CARD!
44
45
PICK A CARD!
PICK A CARD!
41
40
39
38
37
36
29
30
31
33
34
35
PICK A CARD!
32
28
27
26
25
23
22
24
15
16
17
18
20
PICK A CARD
PICK A CARD!
14
13
12
11
10
8
PICK A CARD!
9
1
2
3
4
5
6
7
START
PICK A CARD!

Mit so einer Briefumschlagklammer kannst du die Zeiger befestigen.

4 Word power: Who is the star?

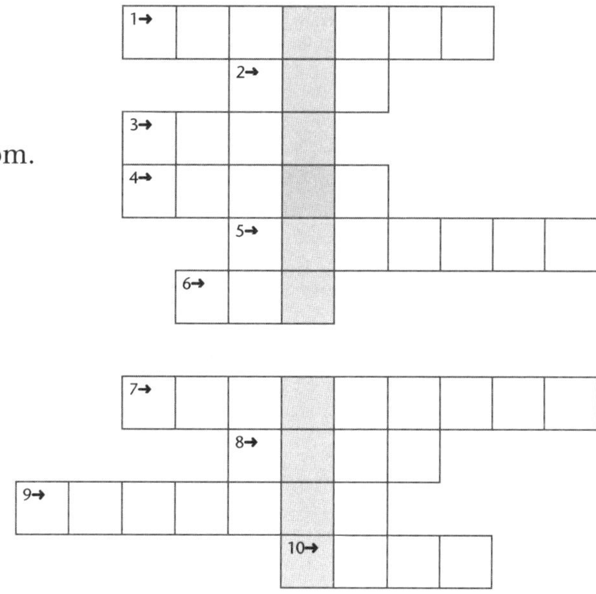

1. Maths is a school …
2. You can see animals here.
3. People do this in the bathroom.
4. English money: £.
5. English school clothes.
6. In a shop you can … things.
7. A school for little children.
8. Seven days.
9. Your mother's father.
10. A little horse.

b) Can you use all the words to tell a little story? Let the class check!

5 The Brown sisters (PB p. 53/ex. 2)

The Brown sisters do lots of things together after school and at the weekend. Write your sentences in your exercise book.

You can start like this:
On Mondays the Brown sisters watch …

make • ride • go • play • have • meet • watch

Monday	Tuesday	Wednesday	Thursday	Friday	Saturday	Sunday
video	bikes	dinner for parents	guitar	friends	shopping	lunch in restaurant

6 Something different

Say what these people ***usually, often*** or ***sometimes*** do in the week and what is different this week. Write your sentences in your exercise book.

Example: 1. Becky usually plays computer games on Tuesday afternoon, but this Tuesday she's doing her homework.

1. play • Becky • usually • afternoon • computer games • Tuesday	**but**	homework • do
2. often • cinema • Mrs Croft and Robert • go • Saturday		restaurant • dinner • have
3. play • evening • usually • Monday • guitar • David		scooter • ride • Robert's
4. morning • breakfast • Jenny • Sunday • make • sometimes		bed • stay
5. weekend • the Burtons • often • picnics • go		work • home
6. Mrs Dixon • fetch • sometimes • Kim and Sarah • shopping centre • Saturday		bus • get • home
7. look at • after • book • often • kindergarten • Mark		watch • TV

Happy birthday

1 The right words (PB p. 62/ex. 1)

Put in the right words in the list.

a) first second ______ third ______ ______ sixth

______ eighth ______ ______

______ twelfth ______ ______

fifteenth ______ seventeenth ______

______ ______

b) ______ ______ ninety-third ______

______ ninety-sixth ______ ______

______ ______

2 When are their birthdays? (PB p. 62/ex. 2)

Find the different people's birthdays and write the dates. Look at the example.

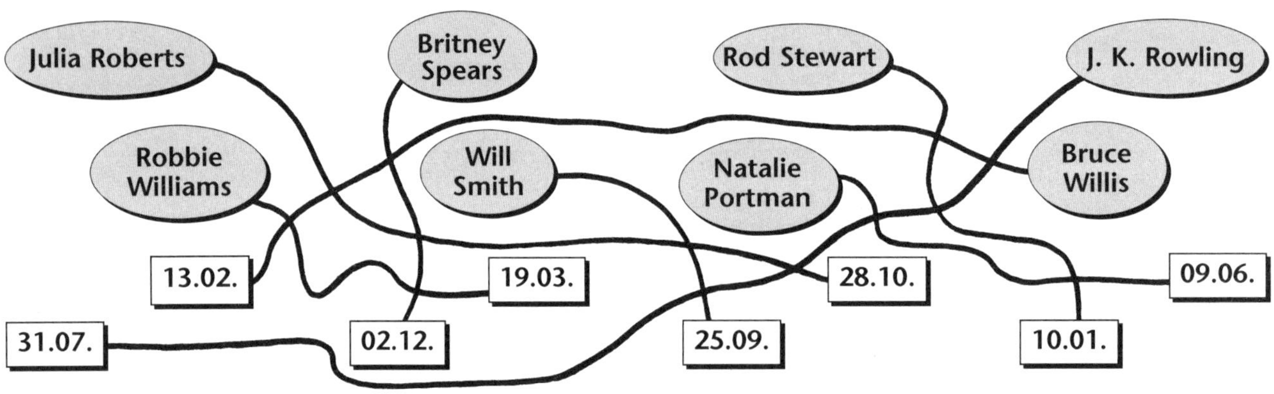

Julia Roberts's birthday is on 28th October.

______

______

______

______

______

______

______

My birthday is on ______

61 3 Can you come to my party? (PB p. 62 / ex. 3)

Listen to the CD and put the missing information in the invitation cards.

4 Birthdays (PB p. 63 / ex. 4)

Put in the right words and find out what the different people are saying about birthdays.

On my birthday I always ____________ my friends to my house.

I love ____________ things like cake and ice cream at birthday parties.

I always write my friends' birthdays in my ____________.

I like birthday parties because there is always a birthday cake with ____________ on it.

On your birthday people sometimes ____________ you the bumps in England. The last bump is for ____________.

Birthday presents are great, but then you must write all those ____________ ____________.

5 Word power: A puzzle (PB p. 63 / ex. 5)

Find nine words and write them next to the puzzle.

C	I	N	V	J	L	M	O	X	Q	S
Y	R	I	B	E	F	O	O	D	I	I
C	A	C	A	L	E	N	D	A	R	B
W	H	A	P	P	Y	T	C	T	E	K
A	L	N	E	A	V	H	A	E	L	O
I	C	D	Y	R	C	A	K	E	I	R
E	X	L	U	M	M	U	C	H	H	O
S	S	E	C	O	N	D	U	M	E	J

→ 1. Food
2. Happy
3. Cake
4. Second
5. ____________
6. ____________
↓ 7. ____________
8. ____________
9. ____________

1 Jenny's birthday (PB p. 64 / ex. 1)

Read the text ***Jenny's birthday*** again and answer the questions. Write short answers.

1. Does Jenny always do something nice on her birthday? ____________________
2. Does she usually go to a restaurant with her family? ____________________
3. Do Jenny's friends give her presents on her birthday? ____________________
4. Do German children have candles on their birthday cakes? ____________________
5. Does Jenny's mum make her birthday cake? ____________________
6. Does Jenny's grandma live near her? ____________________

2 Your birthday (PB page 64 / ex. 1)

Write what you do and what you don't do on your birthday. The pictures can give you some ideas. Look at the example. Be ready to talk about this in class.

On my birthday I always have a birthday cake, but I don't have a party.

____

____

____

____

____

____

____

____

____

____

3 A silly person (PB p. 65 / ex. 3)

This person does not like birthdays. What are the questions to his answers?

1. What's your name? ______
   – My name's No. James No.
2. ______
   – I live in No Man's Lane.
3. ______
   – It's on 29th February. But I hate birthdays.
4. ______
   – I've got no relatives, so I never get birthday cards.
5. ______
   – No, I don't. I never invite friends because I've got no friends.
6. ______
   – No, I never go to a restaurant.
7. ______
   – No, I don't. I never have parties.
8. ______
   – No, I don't. I hate sweet things.

4 Have you got the right answer? (PB p. 65 / ex. 5)

Write short answers to the questions and find out how good you are.

1. Is Berlin a city in England? ______
2. Can Kylie Minogue sing? ______
3. Do English pupils go to school at 7 o'clock? ______
4. Has Madonna got children? ______
5. Does the month of February have 31 days? ______
6. Are Boris Becker and Steffi Graf English? ______
7. Have all flats got gardens? ______
8. Do English children wear school uniform? ______
9. Can cats bark? ______
10. Is David Beckham good at football? ______

Answers: 2, 4, 8 & 10 = yes   1, 3, 5, 6, 7 & 9 = No   You get one point for each right answer. No points for a wrong answer.
10 points = You are brilliant!   9–8 = Very good   7–6 = OK   5–1 = Not very good   0 = Ooops!

1 Party fun (PB p. 66 / ex. 2)

Match the sentences and have fun.

1) Why are there so many Smiths in the telephone book? → b)	a) A hot dog
2) What do you call a dog outside in the sun?	b) They must all have telephones.
3) When is it OK to drink from a plate?	c) Because you can't shut the door.
4) How do you know when your friend has got a secret?	d) Because the bed doesn't come to you.
5) Why do you go to bed?	e) When you're a cat.
6) How do you know there is a monster in the cupboard?	f) Because he or she tells you.

2 The Penroses (PB p. 67 / ex. 3)

Write questions and answers about the Penroses and Jenny. Look at the example.

Questions

How · Who · What · When · Where

~~Penroses • live?~~
Jenny • get up?
David and Jenny • get • school?
take • Mark • kindergarten?
David • do • after school?
Jenny • meet • Saturday afternoon?
David and Jenny • go • bed?

Answers

~~Nottingham~~ · friends · guitar · 8 o'clock in the morning · Mr Penrose · 10.00 · walk

Where do the Penroses live? – They live in Nottingham.

Tipp

Wenn du neue grammatische Lernstoffe mit Buntstiften markierst, z. B. durch Unterstreichen, Durchstreichen, Ausmalen, Zeichnen von Pfeilen ➜ , Umkringeln, Malen von Kästchen usw., kannst du sie dir besser merken. Wie könntest du z. B. deine Fragen in Übung 2 so markieren, dass du dir die Wortstellung in Fragen besser merken kannst?

3 Who or whose? (PB p. 67 / ex. 4)

Look at the answers and write the questions. Start your questions with ***who*** or ***whose***.

1. ______________________________? – Oh, that's my book. Thanks.
2. ______________________________? – I can make lovely cakes.
3. ______________________________? – Yes, please! We all want an ice cream.
4. ______________________________? – It's Anil's birthday party.
5. ______________________________? – I've got a pen. Here you are.
6. ______________________________? – That's Sarah's new bike.

The birthday party

text

1 The birthday party (PB p. 69 / ex. 1)

What happens in the story? Find the sentences and write them in your exercise book in the right order.

1. Everybody at the party is having fun,
2. When Jenny meets Mr Penrose in the hall,
3. They bump Jenny down on the floor
4. Becky, Sarah and David are talking about Jenny's party,
5. Jenny throws the birthday cake in David's face,
6. Suddenly Jenny's friends grab her arms and legs
7. Before Jenny goes to sleep,
8. On the last bump the children let go
9. Jenny suddenly wakes up because

a) and Jenny flies into a huge bowl of trifle.
b) but they stop because Jenny comes in.
c) and throw her in the air.
d) a hand is shaking her.
e) she asks him about the bumps.
f) but Jenny isn't very happy.
g) and hurt her.
h) she worries about the bumps.
i) and then everybody starts to fight.

2 Birthday puzzle (PB p. 69 / ex. 1)

Put in the right words in the puzzle and find the name of Rick Mansfield's group.

1. There's lots of nice food at Jenny's party, but she isn't ___.
2. Jenny doesn't ___ they have the bumps in Germany.
3. While Jenny sleeps, she ___.
4. When the children smile at Jenny, she can see their big white ___.
5. The children ___ poor Jenny's arms and legs.
6. ___ is happy at the party, but Jenny worries about the bumps.
7. ___ throws a jelly at Sarah.
8. David gets trifle on his ___.
9. The children make plans for the party while Jenny is ___.

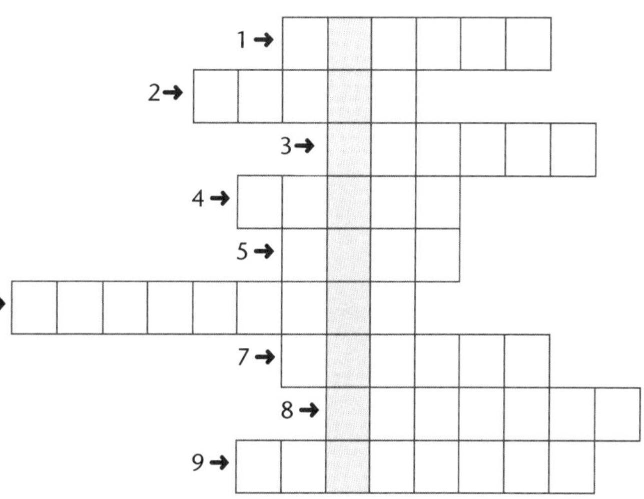

63 3 'Guess the song' (PB p. 69 / ex. 3)

a) Listen to the CD. Are these sentences right or wrong?

	Right	Wrong
1. Tom King plays music on Radio Two.	☐	☐
2. 'Guess the song' is at twenty past seven every day.	☐	☐
3. Bob Dane knows the answer.	☐	☐
4. He's right. He says, "It's Madonna".	☐	☐
5. Rita is from London.	☐	☐
6. Rita wins a CD player.	☐	☐

b) Now correct the wrong sentences.

let's check

1 The day before Jenny's birthday (PB p. 70 / ex. 1)

Everybody in the Penroses' house is busy. Mark is asking everybody questions. Look at the pictures and write Mark's questions. Then write the answers to his questions in your exercise book.

(who • phone)

1. Who are you

(what • make)

2.

(when • be)

3.

(whose • be)

4.

(how • start)

5.

(why • not play)

6.

2 Mixed bag: The *Twenty Questions* game

(PB p. 70 / ex. 2)

It is Jenny's birthday party. The children are playing ***Twenty Questions***. Put in the missing words.

Sarah: Is ______ a thing?

Robert: No, it ______. First question.

Mark: Is it a person?

David: It ______ be a person if it isn't a ______, silly!

Robert: Yes, it is. ______ question.

Jenny: Is he a man?

Robert: No, she's a ______. ______ question.

Becky: ______ she a tennis player?

Robert: No, she ______. ______ question.

Sarah: ______ she sing?

Robert: Er, I ______ think so. Well, that's not her job. Fifth question.

Mark: ______ does she do then?

Robert: Sorry, Mark, but you ______ ask that question. The ______ must be 'yes' or 'no'.

Mark: Oh, OK. Then, ______ she like children?

David: Oh, Mark! Another silly ______.

Robert: Oh, no, it ______. Yes, she ______ children and children really like her. ______ question.

Becky: ______ she on TV?

Robert: Yes, sometimes she's on TV. ______ question.

Mark: ______ she write books?

Robert: Yes, Mark, she ______. ______ you know her name?

Mark: Yes, I ______! It's J.K. Rowling!

Robert: Brilliant, Mark!

3 Stop and think (PB p. 71 / ex. 7)

Can you find answers to these four questions?

1. How can you walk into a room with two legs and walk out again with six legs?

______

2. There is a green house, a blue house and a white house. The green house is on the left and the blue house is on the right. Where is the white house?

______

3. Katharina's brother has got five sisters:
• Lele • Lala • Lulu • Lolo •
What is the name of the fifth sister?

• ______

4. You are having a race. You are third. You run past the person in second place. Where are you now?

______

focus 3 Focus on the UK

1 Tourist attractions[1] in the UK (PB p. 72 / ex. 1)

Newquay Harbour | ~~Big Ben~~ | Loch Ness | Giant's Causeway | Snowdon

Match the names with the pictures.
Find out where these places are in the UK:

1. Big Ben
England

2.

3.

4.

5.

2 At Madame Tussaud's[2] in London (PB p. 72 / ex. 2)

Listen to the group of people outside Madame Tussaud's and write the answers to the questions in your exercise book.

1. What can you see at Madame Tussaud's?
2. Why does Kevin's mum need a camera?
3. How much are the tickets?
4. How much does Madame Tussaud's spend on each famous person?
5. What do many famous people give Madame Tussaud's?
6. When can the group meet outside again?

3 A tourist attraction in your country (PB p. 73 / ex. 3)

a) Make a poster about a tourist attraction in your country. You can work alone or in groups. Find photos or pictures of the place, or draw your own pictures. Give information about …

- where the place is
- how you can get there
- when the place is open / days and times
- what you can see and do there
- how much the tickets are

b) Use your poster to present[3] your tourist attraction to the class.

Tipp
Beim Vortragen musst du daran denken, dass deine Zuhörer deinen Text noch nicht kennen. Sprich langsam und vergiss nicht, zwischendurch am Satzende Luft zu holen.

[1] [ˌtʊərɪst‿ə'trækʃn] – Touristenattraktion • [2] [ˌmædəm tʊ'sɔːdz] • [3] [prɪ'zent] – präsentieren

4 Round the United Kingdom game (PB p. 73 / ex. 4)

Play the game with a partner or in a group. This is what you need: 

Go round the United Kingdom. Read what you must do and answer the questions. If your answer is wrong, you must go to the lighthouse. If you are in the lighthouse, you need a six to go back to the start again. If you are not sure about an answer, look at the map in your book or check with your teacher.

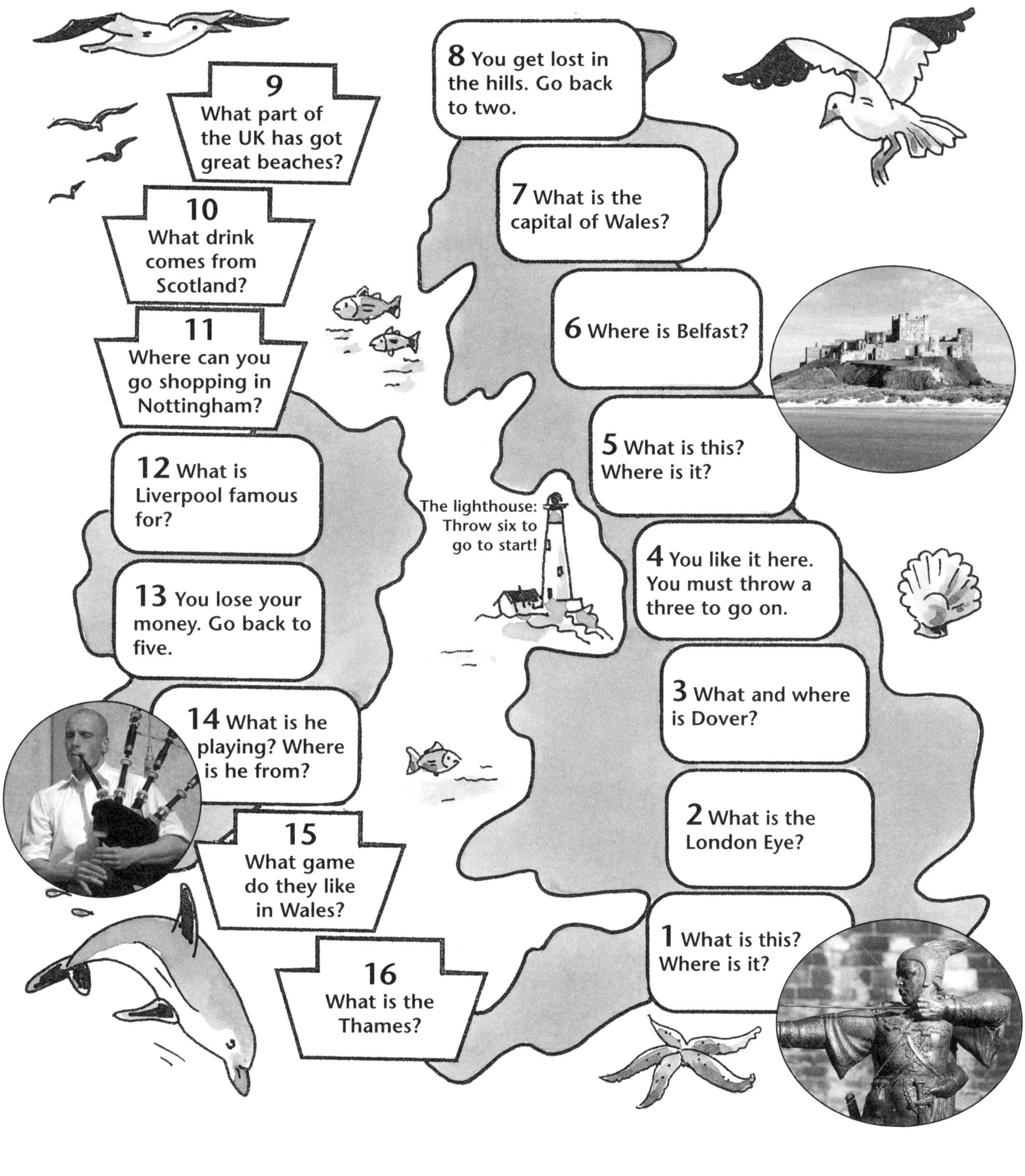

A weekend at the seaside

1 Seaside pictures
(PB p. 74 / ex. 2)

Put in the words and cross out the letters. What letters have you still got? Make another word with them and draw a picture.

A A A A B B
C C D E E E I
L L M M N O
P R R S S T U

bird

Ice cream

2 Ideas for things to do (PB p. 74 / ex. 2)

Use these ideas and finish the dialogues.

Let's ...
Well, we can ...
Why don't we ...

take a boat to the Farne Islands
go to Bamburgh Castle
spend a day on the beach
walk to the harbour
find a café

1. I like boats.

2. I think castles are interesting.

3. I love to swim in the sea.

4. It's fun to watch birds.

5. I'm tired. I want to sit and have a drink now.

3 Where you live (PB p. 74 / ex. 2)

Write a short text for an Internet page about the place where you live.

4 New words (PB p. 74 / ex. 2)

The grey words are new, but you can guess them.
Think of another word from that word family and finish the sentence.

1. A sandy beach has lots of ___sand___. 2. When you ______ a place, you are a visitor. 3. A good swimmer can ______ a long way. 4. In rainy weather, it ______ all the time. 5. If you own a boat, it is your ______ boat. 6. A ______ must never go to sleep while he or she is driving. 7. A birdwatcher finds it interesting to ______ birds. 8. An exciting trip makes you very ______.

On the beach

language A

1 It must be true (PB p. 76 / ex. 2)

What do the pictures tell you? Make sentences with ***must*** be.

cold, sun, music, ice cream ✔, hot, yummy, loud, water

1

2

3

4

1. The ice cream must be ______
2. ______
3. ______
4. ______

2 *Must – needn't* (PB p. 77 / ex. 3)

The Dixons are talking about their trip to Seahouses this weekend. Put in the right word.

1. *Mrs Dixon:* We can go on Friday evening, so Eddy ______ finish work early.
   Sarah: Oh, but I don't want to wait until the evening.
2. *Mr Dixon:* You ______ do all your homework before the weekend, girls.
   Sarah: I needn't. My teachers say I can do it after the weekend.
3. *Mrs Dixon:* We ______ take lots of clothes for just two days.
   Sarah: Maybe not you and Dad and me. But Kim always takes all her things.
4. *Mrs Dixon:* We ______ stop for dinner on the way to Seahouses.
   Mr Dixon: Really? But it's a long way. What if we get hungry?
5. *Sarah:* While we're in Seahouses, we ______ go to the Farne Islands.
   Mrs Dixon: Yes, I'm sure that's an interesting trip.
6. *Kim:* You ______ remember to take your bird book, Dad.
   Mr Dixon: Good idea. Then I can give you information about the birds.

3 *Mustn't – needn't* (PB p. 77 / ex. 3)

The Dixons have got rooms in Mrs Brown's bed and breakfast place. Find the right words and finish what Mrs Brown says.

stand on the yellow lines ✔ | eat there | go to a restaurant | talk so much | get up early | stop and ask people

1. Your car is OK in the street, but it mustn't stand on the yellow lines.
2. You can have breakfast until 10 o'clock. So you ______
3. I can make you sandwiches for your lunch. Then you ______
4. The food in the café next to the bookshop is terrible. You ______
5. Here's a map of Seahouses. Now you ______
6. Of course you want to go upstairs to your rooms. Sorry – I ______

4 Voices in Seahouses (PB p. 77 / ex. 4)

Put in: ***can – can't – must – mustn't – needn't***

1. Excuse me. ______ you tell me the way to the harbour, please? – Sorry, I don't live here, so I ______. You ______ ask another person.
2. Why ______ I have another ice cream? – After three ice creams you ______ ask me that. You ______ know the answer already.
3. Shsh! Dad is sleeping. He ______ be tired. You ______ wake him up. – But there are lots of other noisy children on the beach. So why ______ I be quiet?
4. Look! ______ you read what it says in the window? You ______ bring dogs into my shop. – OK, OK! You ______ shout. I ______ hear you. I'm sure there's another shop where I can spend my money!

5 Questions (PB p. 77 / ex. 4)

Look at the answers. What can the questions be? Think of good ideas.

1. ______? – Yes, I can. That's easy.
2. ______? – No, you mustn't. It's too cold.
3. ______? – No, I can't. But I want to learn.
4. ______? – Oh yes! Then I needn't do it.

A souvenir of the castle

1 What the Dixons say (PB p. 78 / ex. 2)

Put in ***some*** or ***any***.

1. *Mr Dixon*: I'm hungry. I need ______________ food.
2. *Mrs Dixon*: Can you see ______________ restaurants in the street?
3. *Sarah*: Have you got ______________ idea what time the boat goes?
4. *Kim*: Look. Here's ______________ information about the boats.
5. *Mrs Dixon:* Maybe you can find ______________ other young people on the beach, girls.
6. *Sarah*: Kim isn't very happy. There aren't ______________ nice boys in Seahouses.

2 Word power: In other words (PB p. 79 / ex. 4)

Go on with the other sentences.

a lot of | not much | not many | no

1. The beach is very small. There isn't much sand.
2. You can have fun here. ______________
3. The roads aren't very busy today. ______________
4. The harbour is empty. ______________
5. The picnic bag is full. ______________
6. I can't sit here and listen to music. ______________

65 3 Shopping (PB p. 79 / ex. 5)

a) Before the Dixons go to Seahouses, Mrs Dixon needs some things from the shop. Listen and write down what she wants.

____

____

____

b) Look at what Sarah is buying at the shop. What is wrong? Finish the sentences.

1. She has got too ______________
2. There are only ______________
3. There is ______________
4. Mrs Dixon doesn't want ______________

4 Phrases with *of* (PB p. 79 / ex. 6)

Go on with the sentences. Use *of*.

the island | the book | the street | the week | the castle

1. I like the weekend. It's my favourite time of the week.
2. Where does this boat go? What's the name ______
3. Mrs Brown can give you bed and breakfast. Her house is at the end ______
4. Hey, stop that, boys! You mustn't write your names on the walls ______
5. There's a nice picture of some seals. You can see it on the last page ______

5 Watch out (PB p. 79 / ex. 6)

Write sentences with: *'s – s' – of.*

1. The man has got a nice dog. The man's dog is nice.
2. The church has got an interesting door. ______
3. The Dixons have got wet towels. ______
4. The children have got huge ice creams. ______
5. The sea has got a lovely sound. ______
6. Sarah has got new jeans. ______

text

Grace Darling

1 A Grace Darling puzzle (PB p. 82 / ex. 2)

a) Find the words and put them in the right place in the puzzle. (The number of letters can help you.)

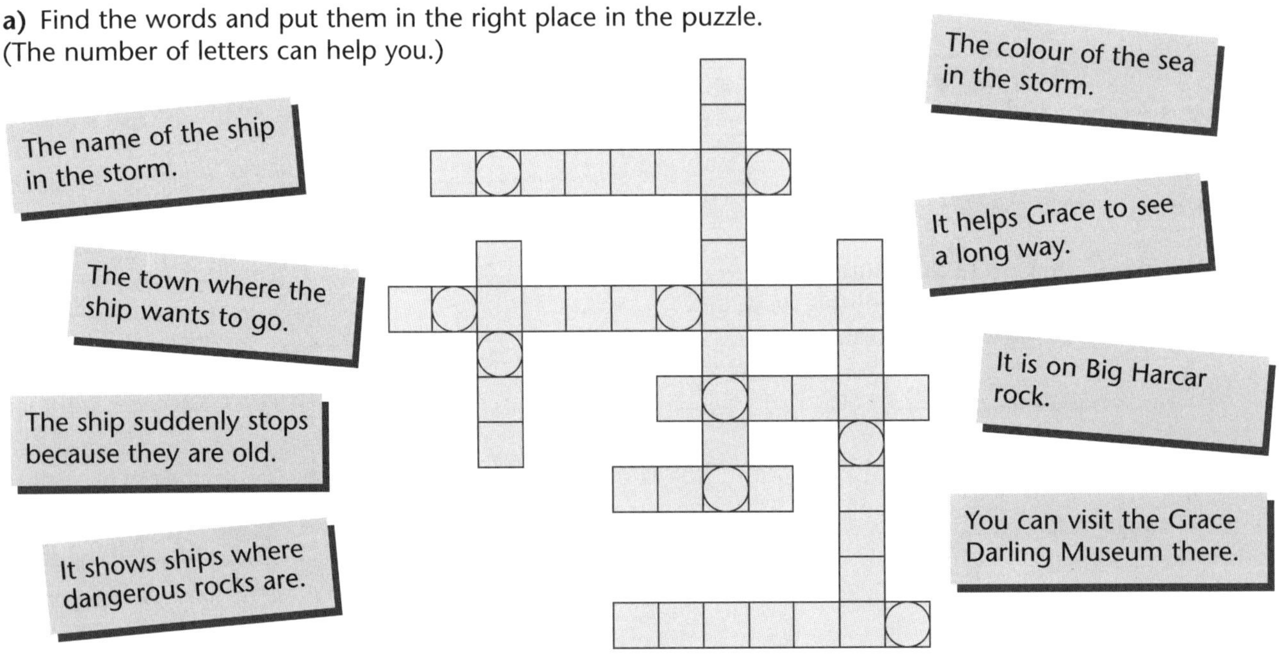

b) Use the letters in the circles and write the name of a place in Northumbria. _ _ _ _ _ _ _ _ _

2 Word pairs (PB p. 82/ex. 2)

Find eight word pairs. Write them in your exercise book. Example: quiet — loud

~~quiet~~ • near • small • empty • ~~loud~~ • big • slow • boring • fast • far • safe • dangerous • new • full • interesting • old

3 British weather (PB p. 82/ex. 4)

a) Write what is happening in this scene.

____

____

____

____

____

____

b) Now go on and write what suddenly happens. Remember to connect your sentences.

____

____

____

____

4 The Grace Darling Museum (PB p. 82/ex. 2)

66

Listen to what Mrs Brown tells the Dixons, then answer the questions.

1. When is the museum open? ______________________________
2. What can you find in the museum? ______________________________

____

____

3. What does everybody want to see? ______________________________
4. How can you find the museum? ______________________________

____

5 Sounds and spelling (PB p. 82 / ex. 2)

Which letters can't you hear when you say the word? Cross the letters out.

talk answer castle island chocolate mustn't wreck listen scene

Tipp

Es gibt viele Wörter, die sich in beiden Sprachen ähnlich schreiben – aber eben doch nicht genau gleich. Fange Karteikarten an und markiere die Unterschiede in der Schreibung, z. B. S<u>z</u>ene – s<u>c</u>ene. Das hilft dir, Fehler zu vermeiden.

6 Can they guess? (PB p. 82 / ex. 4)

Look at the pictures in your book before page 82. Find a nice drawing or photo and say what is happening in the picture. If there are people in the picture, think what they are doing or saying. Be ready to talk about your picture in class. Can the others in your class guess which picture it is?

Think about: where it is → what the scene looks like

who is there → what they are doing → what they usually do

who is there → what they are saying

____

____

____

____

____

7 Mixed bag (PB p. 82 / ex. 4)

The Dixons are in Seahouses on Sunday morning. Put in the missing words.

1. *Sarah*: Look! We ________ get bikes for ________ here!
2. *Kim*: What ________ you want to ________ with a bike?
3. *Sarah:* ________ it, of ________, stupid!
4. *Mr Dixon*: Sarah, please ________ talk to ________ sister like that.
5. *Sarah:* Well, ________ always ________ silly questions. Think about it. We want to ________ to Bamburgh Castle today. So why ________ we go on bikes?
6. *Mrs Dixon:* Sorry, Sarah, but ________ we get bikes, we must bring ________ back at the end ________ the afternoon. And ________ our trip to Bamburgh we don't want to come back here. It ________ the best road for us on our ________ home.

1 Do what I tell you (PB p. 83 / ex. 2)

Write the ideas again with different words. Use: ***must – mustn't – needn't.***

1. Hey, don't throw sand in the picnic bag! You mustn't ______
2. Tell me where you're going. You ______
3. It's OK if you don't come with us. ______
4. You don't want to wear shoes? That's fine. ______
5. No! It's dangerous to play on wet rocks. ______
6. Here's the telescope – but look after it. ______

2 *Some – any* (PB p. 83)

Finish the sentences with ***some*** or ***any*** and one of the words.

pictures | music | sunscreen | secrets | free time

1. The sun is very strong today. I think I need ______
2. Sorry, I can't meet you tomorrow. I haven't got ______
3. Why do people talk so much on the radio? Isn't there ______
4. It's a lovely place. If you like, I can show you ______
5. I tell my best friend everything. We don't have ______

3 *How much? – How many?* (PB p. 83)

1. ______ sandwiches are there?
2. ______ water have we got?
3. ______ boats are in the harbour?
4. ______ are the boat tickets?
5. ______ towels do we need?
6. ______ pocket money do you get?

4 A word quiz (PB p. 83)

What is ***it*** in the sentences? Write the answers in the box.

1. When you look at ***it***, you remember your trip.
2. ***It*** is like a big cup without a saucer.
3. You want to do ***it*** when you are hungry.
4. You need ***it*** when you are wet.
5. ***It*** can be sunny, wet or cold.
6. ***It*** can fly – but it isn't a plane.
7. You must do ***it*** if your boat doesn't have an engine.
8. When boats are in ***it***, they are safe.

1. ______ 5. ______
2. ______ 6. ______
3. ______ 7. ______
4. ______ 8. ______

revision 3
Unit 4 – Unit 5

1 Questions and answers

a) Jack, an English boy, is visiting your school. He asks you some questions. Write them down. Your answers are on the right.

1. Are you thirteen ? – No, I'm not.
2. ______________________ ? – Yes, I can.
3. ______________________ ? – Yes, we do.
4. ______________________ ? – No, we haven't.
5. ______________________ ? – Yes, he has.
6. ______________________ ? – No, she doesn't.
7. ______________________ ? – No, it isn't.

b) Now you ask Jack some questions. Use the words in the boxes. You can find his answers in the pictures. Write your questions and Jack's answers in your exercise book.

where • how • when • what • how many • who

get up • live • brothers and sisters • after school • get to school • pop group

1

2

3

4

5

6

2 Word power: Make new words

Use the words from the boxes and make new words.
Watch out! Put them in the right lists.

air ✓ pencil ✓ every up with invitation shop mouse light sea ice swimming

side out mat assistant case ✓ cream house pool stairs thing port ✓ card

airport
____
____
____
____
____

pencil case
______________ ______________
______________ ______________
______________ ______________
______________ ______________
______________ ______________

3 Signs[1]

Where do you find these signs? Match the places with the pictures. Then write in your exercise book what you ***can, can't, must, mustn't*** and ***needn't do*** in these places.

SEAVIEW HOUSE [b]
◆ two minutes from the beach
◆ TV in every room
◆ dogs are welcome

GET YOUR BOATS HERE! [ ]
£6 for a morning/an afternoon
£10 for a day

Rainbow Theatre [ ]
★ Tickets £1.50
★ Free for children under eight

WHITE SANDS [ ]
☛ Parents, please look after your children in the water.
☛ No loud music, please.
☛ Please be tidy on the beach.

SORRY – NO ICE CREAM TODAY! [ ]

SOUVENIRS [ ]
Open: 9am - 5pm

a) in a café window
b) at a bed & breakfast place
c) on the beach
d) at the harbour
e) at a children's theatre
f) at a souvenir shop

[1]sign [saɪn] – Schild

4 People on the beach

What are these people saying? Put in the words: ***some, any, a lot of, no, many.***

1. Mum, have you got ______ water?
   Of course. There are ______ bottles in the bag.
2. There's ______ sun here. Let's go over there.
   Yes, that's a good idea, and there aren't so ______ people there.
3. Oh Dad, I'm cold and there are ______ towels in the bag!
   I think your sister has got ______ in her bag.
4. We're hungry Mum. Have you got ______ sweets, please?
   Sweets? I haven't got ______ sweets, but you can have ______ sandwiches.

5 A sunny afternoon

What is everybody doing on this sunny afternoon? Write the sentences in your exercise book.
Example: 1. Robert and Simon are watching the end of a football game.

1. watch • football • Robert and Simon • end • game
2. new bike • ride • Jack • his brother
3. Helen • castle garden • draw picture
4. car • wash • her parents • Becky
5. swimming pool • their uncle • swim • Anil and Anuja
6. read • David • his book • last page
7. Sarah • her neighbour • go for walk • dog
8. middle • sleep • Barker • living room

A week on a farm

1 A school trip (PB p. 87 / ex. 1)

Read this information for pupils at a school in Manchester. Can you finish the words?

School trip to Nethercott House for Year 7

Have you got old jeans and a pair of w__________? Do you like f__________ air?

Well, come and s__________ a week on a f__________ in Devon!

This is not a h__________. You have to help with the w__________.

But it can be a lot of fun to m__________ the cows and f__________ the other animals.

And you can l__________ how people in the c__________ live.

If you want to k__________ more about this trip, p__________ tell your tutor – NOW!

2 Word power: Odd word out (PB p. 87/ex. 2)

Which is the odd word out? Draw a circle round it. Why do the other words go together?

1. pig • sheep • turkey • cow: They are all animals with __________
2. farm • bookshop • cinema • supermarket: __________
3. article • song • poem • story: __________
4. stable • horse • shed • pigsty: __________
5. month • week • day • holiday: __________

3 On the farm (PB p. 87/ex. 2)

What are they saying or thinking? Can you think of funny ideas?

Robert's postcard from Yorkshire

1 Regular past forms (PB p. 88/ex. 2)

Make past forms and put them in the right lists. Think how you say them!

[d]	[t]	[ɪd]
played	worked	wanted

~~work~~ wait start phone stop need stay ~~want~~ jump worry invite ~~play~~ watch open look

2 Weekends (PB p. 88/ex. 3)

a) Take your exercise book and write about different weekends. The verbs can help you.

Example: 1. The weekend was boring. We wanted to have a picnic, but it rained all the time. So I stayed at home and cleaned my room.

The weekend was ... 1. boring 2. interesting 3. funny 4. terrible 5. brilliant 6. busy

visit play invite rain work talk to help (with) watch show want hate love clean listen to earn laugh look after stay wash phone carry start need walk shout

b) Think of a special weekend and talk about it in class.

3 Irregular past forms (PB p. 89/ex. 4)

a) Look at the list of irregular verbs on page 155 in your book and find the past forms of these pairs of verbs.

1. bring – ________ buy – ________
2. know – ________ fly – ________
3. think – ________ teach – ________
4. say – ________ read – ________
5. see – ________ wear – ________
6. spend – ________ go – ________

b) Now say the pairs of past forms together. What can you say about them?

____

Tipp

Außer der Liste der unregelmäßigen Verben findest du weitere nützliche Informationen, die dir beim selbstständigen Lernen helfen, in deinem Schülerbuch, z. B. im Grammatik- und Vokabularteil.

4 Yesterday (PB p. 89 / ex. 5)

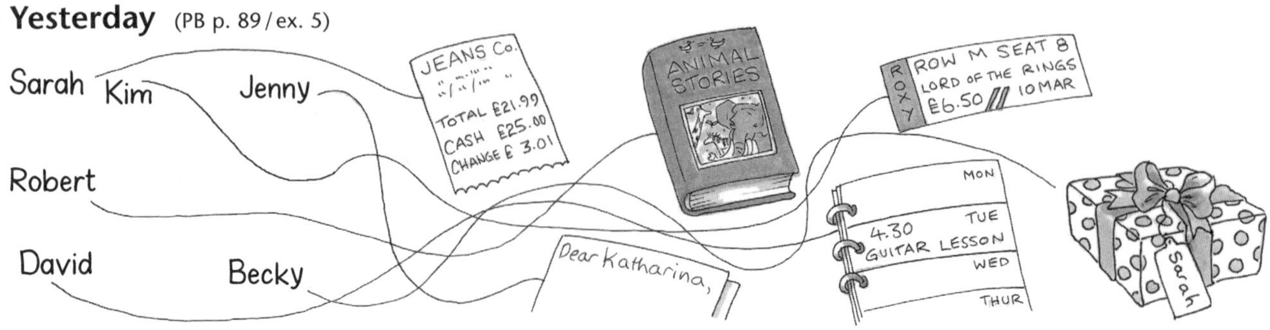

a) What did the friends do yesterday?

1. Kim went to the cinema yesterday.
2. ______________________________
3. ______________________________
4. ______________________________
5. ______________________________
6. ______________________________

b) Your turn: Write some sentences about what you did yesterday. Use your exercise book.

5 Present and past (PB p. 89 / ex. 6)

Find a verb for each sentence pair and put in the correct forms.

be buy listen to watch go have chase feed

1. The Crofts' house __________ in Nottingham, but last week the Crofts __________ on a farm in Yorkshire.
2. When they are in the car, Robert and his mother often __________ music. On the way to Yorkshire last Saturday they __________ Radio One.
3. On Sunday Jack __________ round the farm with Robert. He always __________ round the farm with visitors.
4. Robert usually __________ one egg for breakfast. Yesterday morning he __________ two.
5. In the evenings Jack's parents sometimes __________ TV. Yesterday they __________ a video.
6. This month Jack __________ a new pair of jeans. He often __________ new clothes.
7. Grandpa Rudd usually __________ the chickens, but Jack and Robert __________ them last week.
8. Barker __________ the neighbours' cat again last week. Sam never __________ cats.

1 Questions and answers (PB p. 90/ex. 2)

Put the missing words into the questions. Then answer the questions with short answers.

Did …? Was …? Were …?

1. Did the birds wake you up this morning? Yes, they did./No, they didn't.
2. ______ there a storm where you live yesterday? ______
3. ______ you at school three days ago? ______
4. ______ you and your friends have fun last weekend? ______
5. ______ your room tidy when you went to bed last night? ______
6. ______ you have an egg for breakfast today? ______
7. ______ your teacher happy with your work last year? ______

2 I didn't do it! (PB p. 91 / ex. 5)

Finish the little dialogues.

1. "Who took my magazine?" – "I don't know. I didn't take it."
2. "Who opened my bag of sweets?" – "No idea. ______."
3. "Who used my mobile?" – "Sorry, I can't tell you. But ______."
4. "Who made that noise?" – "Don't look at me. ______."
5. "Who ate all the eggs?" – "Well, ______."
6. "Who threw this ball?" – "I don't know. ______."

3 Robert's dream (PB p. 91 / ex. 6)

Put in past forms. The verbs can help you. Watch out! There are questions and negative forms, too.

be	have	happen	like	dream	think	feed	shout	drink	do

Robert: Hey, Jack! I ______ about you and me and Lenny last night.

Jack: Oh? ______ it a nice dream? What ______ we all ______? Come on, tell me!

Robert: Well, you and I each ______ a bottle of milk. And we ______: "Here, Lenny! Come to me!"

Jack: And whose bottle ______ Lenny ______ better?

Robert: My bottle – because it ______ huge. Your bottle ______ very big.

Jack: So what ______ then? ______ I ______ Lenny after you?

Robert: No, you ______. You ______ your own milk. From the bottle!

Jack: Ha, ha! ______ I ______ I was a little lamb?!

4 Dialogues (PB p. 91 / ex. 7)

Write dialogues. Start with these ideas, then finish the dialogue with a good answer.

1. find a little dog yesterday // what • do with it?

You: I found a little dog yesterday.

Your friend: What did you do with it?

You: ____________________

2. go to bed early last night // why • tired?

You: ____________________

Your friend: ____________________

You: ____________________

3. hurt my head two days ago // how • happen?

You: ____________________

Your friend: ____________________

You: ____________________

4. have an interesting visitor last Saturday // who • visit you?

You: ____________________

Your friend: ____________________

You: ____________________

5 A postcard (PB p. 91 / ex. 7)

You are on holiday. Write a postcard to a friend in English. Say where you are and what you ***did*** or ***didn't*** do there. Here are some ideas:

seaside • farm • island • castle • swimming pool • beach • park • boat • play • go • visit • watch • collect • animals • birds

Dear ____________________

Problems on Springfield Farm

1 How do you feel? (PB p. 93)

a) Explain how you feel. Choose from the words.

scared · hungry · sad · worried · happy · tired · free · surprised · angry · terrible

1. It is the weekend. You needn't go to school again until Monday. You feel ______________.
2. Breakfast was a long time ago – and you didn't eat enough. You feel ______________.
3. Your pet rabbit dies. You feel ______________.
4. A girl said something terrible about you (not true, of course!). You feel ______________.
5. You win a trip to London. You feel ______________.
6. You are on holiday in another country. You meet your teacher. You feel ______________.

b) Which words didn't you use in **a)**? Explain when you feel like this.
Write the sentences in your exercise book. Example: I feel **tired** when I get up early.

2 One sentence from two (PB p. 94 / ex. 1d)

Use the words on the right and connect these sentences. Write the new sentences in your exercise book.

Start: When the Crofts were on Springfield Farm, there was a problem.
Grandpa Rudd came into the kitchen, ...

and · **until** · **when** · **so** · **but** · **because**

1. The Crofts were on Springfield Farm. There was a problem.
2. Grandpa Rudd came into the kitchen. He didn't sit down.
3. He was worried. One of the sheep was in a bad way.
4. They wanted to help the sheep. Mrs Rudd phoned the vet.
5. They waited. The vet came.
6. The vet examined the sheep. He shook his head.
7. He got two lambs out of the mother sheep. They were dead.
8. Robert saw the lambs. He felt terrible.
9. They didn't know how to save the sheep. Robert had a good idea.
10. Grandpa Rudd put the skin of one of the dead lambs around Lenny. He needed the right smell.
11. Grandpa tricked the sheep. Lenny drank from her.
12. Everybody smiled. They were happy.

67 3 Chickens in the city (PB p. 95 / ex. 3)

a) Robert is at Sarah's house. Listen and write notes about what Mrs Dixon says.

When a girl — holiday on farm — loved it — parents, too — fresh eggs

____

____

____

____

b) What happened when Mrs Dixon was a girl? Use your notes from **a)** and write the story in your exercise book.
Start: When Mrs Dixon was a girl, she had a holiday on a farm.
She loved it there, and her parents loved it, too, especially the ...

4 Headlines[1] (PB p. 95 / ex. 3)

Headlines often use present forms – but of course the articles are in the past.
a) Make sentences. In some sentences you must put in the words ***a*** or ***some***.

1. **Friends find bag of money:** Some friends found a bag of money.
2. **CAR HITS BUS:** ______
3. **Star opens new music shop:** ______
4. CUSTOMERS GET SURPRISE: ______
5. Party for 100-year-old: ______
6. **DOG SAVES GIRL:** ______

b) Choose one of the headlines and tell the story to the class.

[1] ['hedlaɪn] – Schlagzeile

5 Another story (PB p. 95 / ex. 3)

Jack told Robert another story about Springfield Farm. Robert likes it so much that he wants to write it down. Can you help him? Use his notes and write the story in your exercise book.

1. Last year • visitors from London • girl, Sally, and her mum • very nice clothes • big car • little dog, Susie
2. Jack liked Sally • she wanted to help on farm, play with Sam and Jack • mother said: "You mustn't help on the farm" • "clothes are getting wet" • "animals are dangerous" • didn't like the farm smells • frightened of Sam • Sally sad, read books inside all the time
3. One evening • mother went for a walk with Susie • suddenly Susie ran away • chased a bird • mother didn't find her • came back sad, cried
4. Jack, Sam and Sally went out • fields • night, dark • old house • Sally frightened • suddenly Sam barked • Susie inside, wanted to get out • door closed • Jack opened door • Susie came out
5. Jack, Sam and Sally took Susie home • "Sam found her" • Sally's mother very happy • "thank you" • gave Jack and Sam a huge present • "of course Sally can play with you and Sam" • rest of holiday great!

6 Poems (PB p. 95 / ex. 4)

Read these two 'city' poems. Then write more poems like this – about the city or the country. Use your exercise book.

7 Which word do you hear? (PB p. 95 / ex. 4)

These word pairs have the same sound. Finish the sentences with one word from each pair.

right – write | hear – here | week – weak | see – sea | buy – by | no – know | there – their

1. Did you come to Yorkshire __________ car? 2. Please have some cake – __________ you are.

3. I'm not __________. I'm very strong! 4. The Rudds often have visitors on __________ farm.

5. Oh, dear! There are __________ eggs today. 6. I must __________ a postcard to my friend.

7. Look! You can __________ the Yorkshire hills from this window.

8 Word power: Say it in other words (PB p. 95 / ex. 4)

If you don't know a word in English, don't worry! You can often explain it in other words. Try to explain these German words.

Example: 1. Verkehrsstau: This happens when there are too many cars.

2. Kalb: __________

3. grunzen: __________

4. Sattel: __________

5. weinen: __________

6. Erbsen: __________

9 Verbs or nouns (PB p. 95 / ex. 4)

Some words can be verbs or nouns. Example: **to visit** is a verb, and **a visit** is a noun.

a) Write these sentences again.

1. Have a **guess** at the answer. Try to guess the answer.
2. I must have a **wash** before dinner. I must __________
3. They gave a **wave** when they saw us. __________
4. Can I have a **ride** on your bike, please? __________
5. We had a long **wait** for the train. __________

b) Now write these sentences again with nouns.

1. I often **dream** at night. I often have dreams at night.
2. Let's **plan** a nice holiday. Let's make __________
3. This egg **smells** bad. __________
4. She **watered** the vegetables. __________
5. They **picnicked** in a field. __________

1 A word puzzle (PB p. 96 / ex. 1)

a) What are the correct letters?

1. You have skin all over your ___ ___ ◯ Y.
2. You feel nervous and ___ ◯ ___ ___ I ___ ___ when you have a problem.
3. When you are happy, you have a ___ M ◯ ___ ___ on your face.
4. If a job is important, you must do it right ___ W ___ ◯.
5. People often go for a walk because they need some ___ R ___ ___ ◯ air.
6. You must open the ___ ◯ ___ E when you want to go into a field.
7. You make an ___ ___ ___ ◯ ___ ___ T ___ with eggs.

b) Use the letters in the circles and write the missing word in this sentence:

Everybody needs a ◯ ◯ ◯ ◯ ◯ ◯ ◯ from time to time.

2 Mixed bag: A pig story (PB p. 96 / ex. 5)

Mrs Rudd is telling the Crofts a story. Put in the missing words.

Two years ________ our ________ Tom Potter wanted to ________ two ________ his pigs to market. So he ________ them to a town not far ________ here. But the pigs ________ want to die. So ________ he got there, they ran ________ the open gate ________ the street. Tom ________ the pigs, but they were ________ fast for ________ – and he didn't ________ them again. Of ________ Tom ________ very happy, and all ________ other people laughed. The story ________ on TV here in Yorkshire! At ________, after many days, a woman ________ the two ________ in her garden. She ________ to save them, so she ________ them from Tom, and now they are ________ pets. So you see, in the ________ the story had a happy ________ for everybody!

3 Questions about school (PB p. 97 / ex. 7)

Mr Penrose always has lots of questions when David gets home from school. What does he ask?

Mr Penrose wants to know ... **He asks David:**

1. ... what David did at school today. What did you ____________________
2. ... what lessons he had. ____________________
3. ... which lesson was best. ____________________
4. ... who played tricks in class. ____________________
5. ... what the teachers said. ____________________
6. ... who David saw after school. ____________________

4 Girls and boys (PB p. 97 / ex. 7)

Write another sentence about each girl and boy. Use these ideas:

not eat much breakfast • love every minute of his holiday there last week • go to bed late yesterday evening • get it from her parents' shop • not remember to buy eggs • not listen in class today

1. Sarah can't do her homework. She didn't ____________________.
2. Mark is tired. He ____________________.
3. Becky has got a new bike. ____________________.
4. Jenny is hungry. ____________________.
5. David must go back to the supermarket. ____________________.
6. Robert wants to visit Springfield Farm again. ____________________

____________________.

5 Yesterday evening (PB p. 97 / ex. 8)

Think what verbs you need and put in the missing past forms.

Robert: What __________ you __________ yesterday evening, David?

David: I __________ TV. __________ you __________ TV, too?

Robert: No. I __________. I __________ my Car Race computer game.

David: Oh yes, that's a good game. And __________ you __________ the race?

Robert: Win it? No, I __________. My car __________ fast enough.

David: You mean, you __________ a good enough driver!

4 focus

Focus on English – a world language

1 What languages can they speak? (PB p. 98 & 99 / ex. 1)

José: Spanish and ____________________

Jörg: ____________________

Vanessa: ____________________

Noreen: ____________________

Hanif: His own language in Delhi and

____

Grace: ____________________

____

2 You know these words (PB p. 99 / ex. 2)

Look at the pictures and put in the English words in the puzzle. You know some of these English words. You know the other words in English because people use them in Germany, too.

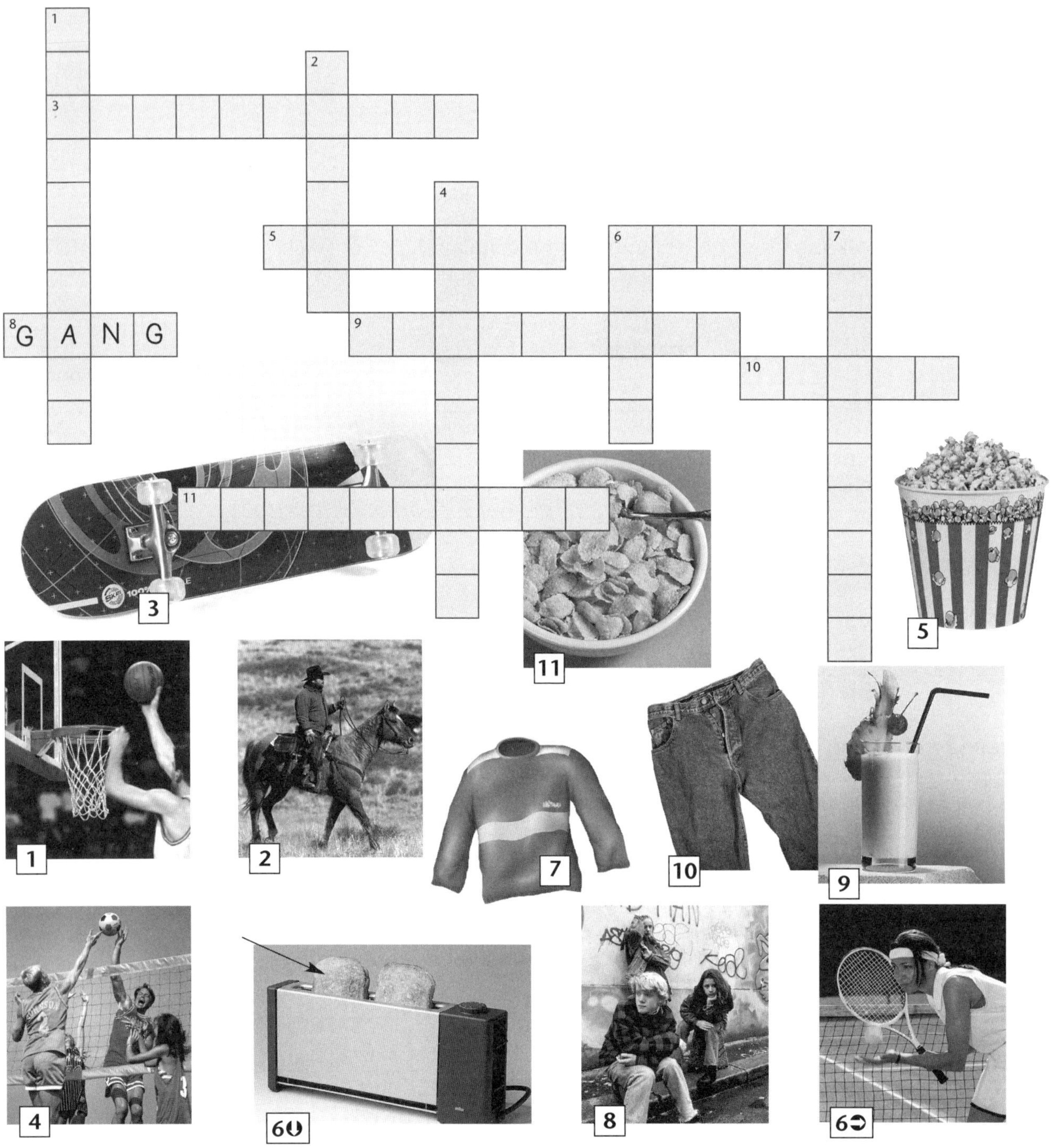

3 A lesson (PB p. 99 / ex. 2)

Put in the right words.

Teacher: It's always good to know more __________ one language. Which language do people in Germany __________, Kevin?

Kevin: They __________ German, but at school they learn English, too, or __________ or sometimes Italian or __________.

Teacher: Yes, that's right. And there are a lot of different German __________ in different parts of the country, too. It's like English: In Scotland it sounds very different from English in London, Ireland or California. In the USA people usually need English, but there are places in the US where people don't __________ it, because many of them come from different countries, for example Mexico and speak a different __________. Do you know why English is so __________?

Jill: I think because people know it almost __________. It's an __________ language! You can use it not only in the UK or the USA, but for example, in South __________, __________ or Australia.

Teacher: Yes, so let's not __________ your English homework! We talked about English words from other languages yesterday. Please show me the __________ with your words and the pictures from magazines.

4 When do people need English? (PB p. 99 / ex. 3)

Finish this mind map with your own ideas.

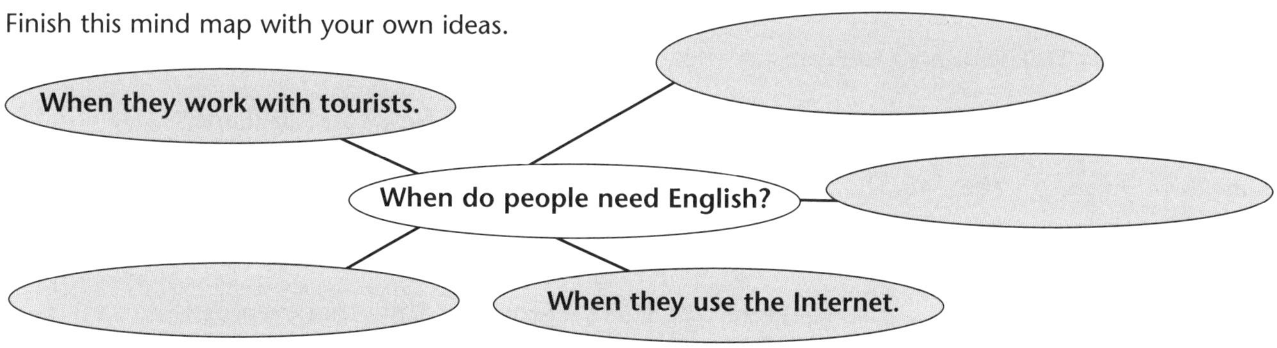

5 English outside school (PB p. 99 / ex. 3)

a) Listen to these children. They're talking about the English language.
Make notes and say how they use their English outside school.

Felix **Demaris** **Piet** **Maria** **Patience**

b) Now write about how you use your English outside school.

Off to the USA!

1 Places on the map (PB p. 101 / ex. 2)

a) Put the missing names in the boxes.

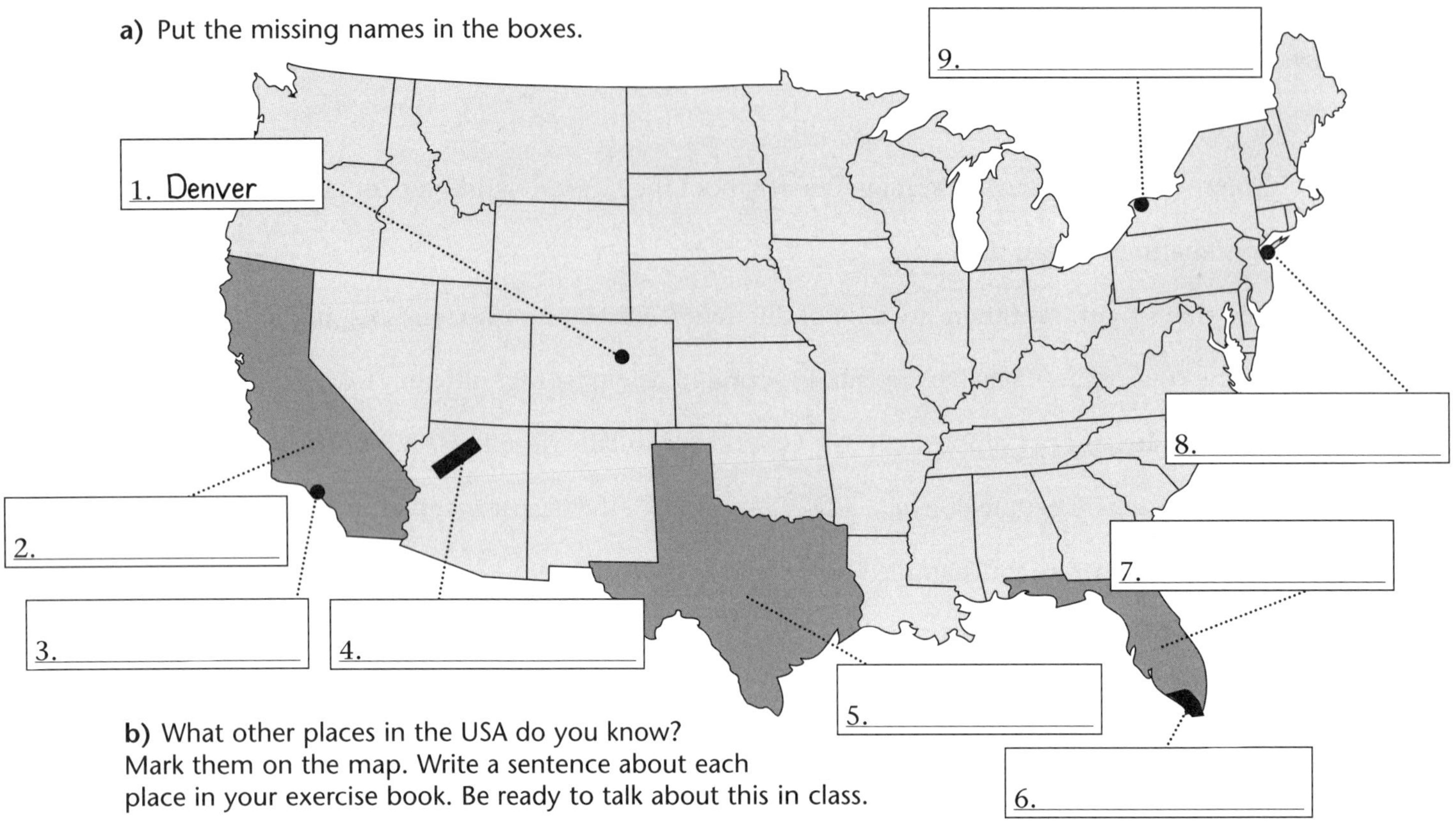

b) What other places in the USA do you know? Mark them on the map. Write a sentence about each place in your exercise book. Be ready to talk about this in class.

2 Brilliant! (PB p. 101 / ex. 2)

David is writing an e-mail to a friend. Put in the missing verbs: ***simple present*** or ***simple past***?

Hey! I'm off to the USA in August! With Mum! She __________ **(tell)** us about it last weekend. It __________ **(be)** Friday evening and we __________ **(be)** all in the kitchen. "I __________ **(have got)** a question for you, David," she __________ **(say)**. "__________ **(you, want)** to come to New York with me? You can stay there with Aunt Meg while I __________ **(fly)** to Denver." For a moment I __________ **(not, say)** anything. "Me? New York? Brilliant!" Mark __________ **(be)** sad. He __________ **(want)** to come with us. Mum __________ (talk) to him: "I __________ **(be)** sorry, Mark. You __________ **(be)** too young. You can come with me when you __________ **(be)** ten. OK? That's a promise." Later that evening I __________ **(look)** at a map of the USA. Suddenly Mum __________ **(come)** into my room. She __________ **(show)** me where New York is. "You can meet your twelve-year-old American cousin at last!" she __________ **(say)**. "Oh, great!" I __________ **(think)**.

David's surprise

1 Plans (PB p. 102 / ex. 2)

What are the children going to do in the summer holidays? Write sentences with ***going to.*** Use these verbs:

drive **fly** **stay** **go skating** **work** **go camping**

1. David is going to ______________________________
2. Sarah ______________________________
3. Kim ______________________________
4. Robert and his mum ______________________________
5. Becky and Sarah ______________________________
6. Mark ______________________________

2 Sounds and spelling (PB p. 103 / ex. 3)

Which word has a different sound? Mark it.

1. [əʊ] don't – boat – go – house
2. [ɪ] fish – knife – milk – pig
3. [æ] dad – happy – late – sand
4. [i:] bed – please – see – week
5. [ɒ] dog – on – phone – watch
6. [aɪ] I've – right – swim – write

3 Word power: Pairs (PB p. 103 / ex. 3)

Find the opposite and write down the word pairs.

1. Which is the **smallest** US state?
   smallest ↔ largest
2. Is Texas in the **north**?
   ____
3. He was there **before** the summer holidays.
   ____
4. That's a **terrible** idea!
   ____
5. 'To visit' is a **regular** verb.
   ____
6. It's **the same** colour.
   ____
7. Do you **remember** your last holiday?
   ____
8. It's a very **poor** country.
   ____

4 Watch out! (PB p. 103 / ex. 3)

1. Watch out, David! (fall over • bag)

You're going to fall over that bag.

2. Watch out, Sarah! (run into • woman)

____

3. Mark, look where you're going! (get lost)

____

4. Come on, Mark and David! (we • be late)

____

5. Watch out, Mum! (lose • ticket)

____

6. The weather is bad. Look at those clouds. (it • rain?)

____

7. You're right. It's starting to rain already! (I • not • stay here)

____

language B

You Brits!

1 I like it (PB p. 104 / ex. 1)

Look at the pictures and write sentences in your exercise book. Use ***like / love* + *...ing.***

Example: I like eating apples. Or: Mary-Beth likes living in the Big Apple.

2 Do you like tennis? (PB p. 105 / ex. 3)

a) Complete this dialogue between Mary-Beth and David. You need four small words.

1. What else do you like doing apart ____________ playing football?

   – Well, I'm interested ____________ tennis.

2. Tennis? Well, how ____________ having a game this afternoon?

   – OK. But don't forget! I'm not very good ____________ tennis. I just like playing.

b) Write a dialogue in your exercise book. Use these words: go to the pool | swim | listen to music

3 Free time (PB p. 105 / ex. 3)

like **be good at** **be interested in**

Write two sentences for each picture, one with the ***present progressive*** and one with a ***gerund***.

1. She's skating.

I like skating.

2. ______

3. ______

4. ______

5. ______

6. ______

4 A puzzle (PB p. 105 / ex. 4)

Put in the right words and their letters and find the answer to the puzzle.

1. Central Park ______ | B
2. Hudson ______ |
3. Empire State ______ |
4. Madison Square ______ |
5. New ______ |
6. South Street ______ |
7. Rockefeller ______ |
8. Statue of ______ |

5 Last summer
(PB p. 105 / ex. 4)

a) Listen and make notes.

	Becky	David	Robert
where they were:	in Nottingham		
what they did:			
what they liked best:			

b) Now ask Kim some questions about her last summer holidays.

1. Where ______________________?
   – Last year? Oh, we went to Italy.
2. ______________________?
   – Oh, we went to the beach every day.
3. ______________________?
   – That's easy! The food. I love pizza! Don't you?
4. ______________________?
   – This year? I'm going to work in a supermarket.

c) Write a short text in your exercise book. Say where you went last summer, what you did, what you liked best and what you are going to do this year.

text

Dead on the roof?

1 Dead on the roof? (PB p. 106–7 Text)

a) Put the sentences in the correct order (1–6) and tell the story again.
b) Write a final sentence for the story.

Tipp
Wenn es in einer Übung darum geht, die richtige Reihenfolge zu finden, ist es wichtig, zuerst alle Wörter oder Sätze durchzulesen. So kommst du leichter auf die Lösung.

__ David thought the man was dead. Perhaps he was a gangster.
__ David was a bit nervous about flying.
__ Suddenly Mary-Beth saw a man on the roof of a skyscraper.
__ Mary-Beth and David went on a sightseeing tour of New York by helicopter.
__ The pilot landed on the skyscraper and talked to the man.
__ First they flew over the Statue of Liberty. Then they flew back to Manhattan.

7 ______________________

____

2 Mixed bag: The pilot talks (PB p. 108 / ex. 3)

The pilot is telling a journalist what happened on the sightseeing tour. Put in the missing words.

"The weather was ______ that afternoon. At about 2.30 the kids got into the ______ and we took off. First we ______ around the ______ of Liberty and Mary-Beth ______ some photos. ______ we went back to Manhattan. Suddenly Mary-Beth ______ a man on the ______ of a skyscraper. We ______ he was dead. Next to him there was a ______ or something. I talked to the ______. I said it was an ______. I landed on the roof and ______ over to the man. His ______ were closed, but he wasn't ______. We gave him some ______ and helped him to stand up. He wasn't a ______, of course. He was a ______, and his 'gun' was an ______!"

3 Sounds and spelling (PB p. 108 / ex. 3)

Which words have the same sound? Put them in the correct boxes. Find one more word for each box.

rain — dead — eye — great — gun — floor — weigh — where

door	fly	late	plane	said	say	ton	their

4 The key[1] (PB p. 108 / ex. 3)

a) Look at the four pictures and collect ideas for a story. Remember: ***Who? Where? When? What?***
b) Write the story in the simple past in your exercise book. Give it a beginning, a middle and an end.
c) Read your story through. Check the grammar, spelling and word order.

[1] [ki:] – Schlüssel

5 Word power: Word groups (PB p. 108 / ex. 4)

Put the words into the correct box and find two more words for each box.

arm • back • dream • excited • journalist • eyes • faint • finger • frightened • funny • gangster • lady • laugh • pilot • smile • worried

people	parts of the body	how people feel	what people do

let's check

1 What is going to happen now? (PB p. 109)

1. David is buying a DVD. He's going to watch it.
2. Robert is giving Sarah a CD . ______
3. Becky has got a camera. ______
4. Mr and Mrs Penrose are carrying tennis rackets. ______
5. Robert and David want to watch a funny video. ______
6. Jenny is looking for her pen. ______
7. Mary-Beth is sitting at her computer. ______

2 Football and music (PB p. 109)

Make questions and answers with gerunds.

1. **(you • like • play)** Do you ______ football?

   – Yes, I **(love • play)** ______ football!

   (how about • meet) ______ in the park this afternoon?

2. **(you • be good at • play)** ______ the guitar?

   – Well, I **(like • make)** ______ music.

   (you • be interested in • play) ______ in our group?

   – Your group? What a good idea! I'm sure **(play)** ______ with you is fun.

3 Mixed bag: I was surprised (PB p. 109)

Mary-Beth is writing an e-mail to a school friend. Put in the right forms.

Hi Britney!

1. Being (be) with David was great fun. I ______ (be) really surprised. Usually boys are so stupid! I really ______ (like, show) him the city. ______ (skate) through Central Park was great. David's not very good at ______ (skate), but he ______ (like, watch) the people in Central Park.

2. In the second week we ______ (watch) the Giants. Two of my friends ______ (come) with us. David ______ (not, understand) everything, but we ______ (help) him, of course. Now he's a real football fan!

3. One day we ______ (go, shop). David was not interested in ______ (look) at clothes. He ______ (want, buy) something for his little brother. It ______ (be) very boring! We ______ (look) at stupid souvenirs all day!

Love, Mary-Beth

4 Word power: Small words (PB p. 109)

Put in the missing prepositions.

1. We're going to stay ______ our uncle in July.
2. I hate sitting in front ______ the TV all day.
3. Are you interested ______ American football?
4. I've got an important message ______ you.
5. She wants to meet us ______ the airport.
6. We're flying from Munich ______ London.
7. What else do you do apart ______ singing?
8. Look! There's a man ______ the roof over there.

5 Word power: Find the missing word (PB p. 109)

1. Great Britain ➜ London
   USA ➜ ______
2. father ➜ mother
   uncle ➜ ______
3. sleep ➜ slept
   meet ➜ ______
4. invite ➜ invitation
   fly ➜ ______
5. classroom ➜ teacher
   plane ➜ ______
6. today ➜ tomorrow
   now ➜ ______
7. fries ➜ chips
   chips ➜ ______
8. leg ➜ foot
   arm ➜ ______
9. tired ➜ sleep
   hungry ➜ ______

Unit 6 – Unit 7

1 Last Saturday

What did the children do last Saturday? Put in the correct forms of the simple past.

1. *Jenny*: Well, I ____________ **(want)** to buy a CD on Saturday, but I ____________ **(not, have)** enough money, so I ____________ **(stay)** in my room and ____________ **(do)** my homework. I ____________ **(finish)** it all before lunch. So I ____________ **(have)** a lot of free time later!

2. *David*: After breakfast I ____________ **(phone)** my grandma. Mark ____________ **(talk)** to her, too. He ____________ **(make)** me really angry because he ____________ **(tell)** her about my last Maths test! It ____________ **(be)** terrible! But later he ____________ **(say)** sorry, and in the afternoon we ____________ **(walk)** to the park and ____________ **(have)** a lot of fun.

3. *Becky*: In the morning I ____________ **(go)** to Sarah's house. We ____________ **(listen to)** some music and ____________ **(talk)** about school. Then we ____________ **(play)** badminton in the garden. Later I ____________ **(help)** Sarah to clean her room!

4. *Robert*: On Saturday I ____________ **(watch)** a funny film on TV. When I ____________ **(go)** to bed, I ____________ **(not, feel)** tired. So I ____________ **(read)** some of my old comics. They ____________ **(be)** really funny, too. On Saturday I ____________ **(get up)** just before lunch!

2 Short answers

1. Were you at school yesterday? No, ____________
2. Did you get up late on Sunday? Yes, ____________
3. Was it cold at the weekend? No, ____________
4. Have you got a pet? No, ____________
5. Are you listening? Yes, ____________
6. Can you milk a cow? No, ____________

3 Jack in Birmingham

A week ago Jack Rudd visited his aunt in Birmingham. Now he's back, and Robert is talking to him.

a) Write down Robert's questions.

1. **(where • you • go?)** ____________
2. **(how long • you • be there?)** ____________
3. **(you • have fun?)** ____________
4. **(what • you • do?)** ____________
5. **(you • be • sad • to come home?)** ____________

b) Write Jack's answers to Robert's questions in your exercise book. Use your own ideas.

4 This afternoon

Where are the children? What are they doing? What are they going to do this afternoon?
Write in your exercise book.

Example: 1. Kim is in bed. She's sleeping. This afternoon she's going to work at the supermarket.

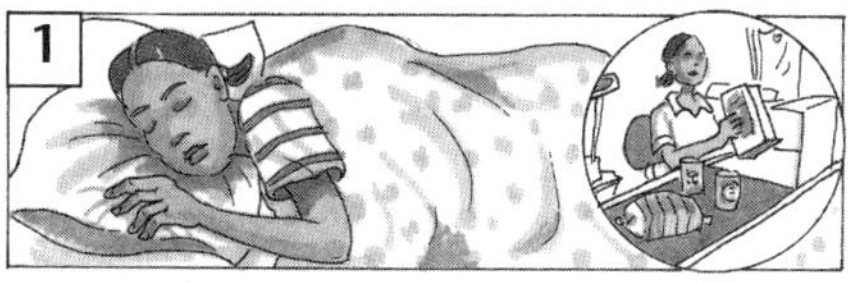

5 See you in September!

This is a postcard from Robert to Sarah. Put in what's missing.

Hi Sarah!

I promised ______ (promise) you a postcard ______ from Scotland, so here it ______ (be)!

We ______ (arrive) in Edinburgh yesterday. The t______ ______ (take[1]) longer than we ______ (think). Why? Well, you know, I'm not very good at ______ (read) m______! Edinburgh's a great p______. My mum ______ (want, go) sightseeing, but I'm more interested in ______ (shop) .

I think it's going to be a great h______! What did you do in France apart from ______ (lie) on the b______? ______ (you, learn) any new F______ words? How about ______ (tell) me about your summer when I get home?
See you in September!
Robert

[1] *hier:* dauern

6 Pairs

Find the other word and make a pair.

1. small or ______	4. beginning and ______	7. dead or ______
2. above or ______	5. open or ______	8. past and ______
3. poor or ______	6. fish and ______	9. with or ______

translation & mediation

1 Der Frosch in der Schachtel (Unit 1 / Text) 

Stell dir vor, du triffst Simon und Becky im Arnot Hill Park.

Du: (begrüßt sie, stellst dich vor und fragst den Jungen, wie er heißt)

____

____

Simon: *My name is Simon. This is Becky. She's my sister.*
Becky: *Where are you from?*
Du: (sagst, wo du herkommst)

____

(und fragst Simon, was er in der Schachtel hat)

____

Simon: *Oh, it's a frog. It's from the park.*
Du: (fragst, warum der Frosch in der Schachtel ist)

____

Simon: *I must put it under that big tree.*
Becky: *Look, it has got friends there.*
Du: (sagst, dass es schöne Frösche sind)

____

Becky: *Yes, they are. Sorry, but we must go now. Bye!*
Du: (verabschiedest dich von Becky und Simon)

____

2 Mit dem Bus nach Sherwood (Unit 2 + Focus 2)

Du bist mit deinem Vater in Nottingham. Ihr steht in Market Square und wollt nach Sherwood fahren.

Vater: Wir wollen mit dem Bus nach Sherwood fahren. Frag mal die Dame da drüben, ob es von hier einen Bus nach Sherwood gibt.

Du: ______________________________

Woman: *Sorry, no idea. But there's a board with information about buses over there.*

Du: Sie weiß es nicht, aber da drüben ______________________________

____

Vater: Ach ja. Danke.

Du: ______________________________

Vater: Frag auch, wo wir Fahrscheine bekommen.

Du: ______________________________?

Woman: *You can get them from the driver.*

Du: ______________________________

Vater: Vielen Dank. Auf Wiedersehen!

Du: ______________________________

Tipp
Beim Dolmetschen musst du nicht alle Wörter ins Englische oder Deutsche übersetzen. Was ist das Wichtigste? Welche Informationen brauchst du unbedingt?

3 An der Haywood School (PB p. 99 / ex. 2)

Katharina erzählt ihrer jüngeren Schwester Susanne, die noch kein Englisch kann, was in Jennys E-mail über die Schule stand. Kannst du ihr helfen?

Tipp

Vergiss nicht: Ein und dieselbe Sache wird in der einen Sprache oft ganz anders ausgedrückt als in der anderen. Wenn es also um die Schule geht, denke daran, wie du normalerweise über die Schule erzählst.

Katharina: Hmm, es ist dort an der Schule anders. Oh ja: *„We wear school uniform and we have lunch at school."*
Susanne: Was heißt das?

Katharina: Sie tragen ____________________ und ____________________

____

Susanne: Was essen sie denn?
Katharina: Das sagt sie nicht. Aber das ist schon besser: *„I never get up before 8 o'clock in the morning".*

Also: Sie ____
Susanne: Wann fängt die Schule denn an?
Katharina: Na, wo stand das, wann sie anfangen? Ach ja, davor: *„We start at 8.45 every day".*

____

Susanne: Das ist aber spät. Dann machen sie auch spät Schluss, oder?
Katharina: Ja, was meinst du? Hier steht *„Lessons finish at half past three."*

____

Susanne: Um halb vier erst? Dann haben sie aber keine Hausaufgaben, so wie du!
Katharina: Doch, doch. Hier steht's: *„After school we usually go home and do our homework".* Also:

____

____

4 Ryans Party (Unit 4 + Focus 3)

Du rufst bei deinem englischen Bekannten Ryan an, um ihm zum Geburtstag zu gratulieren. Deine Mutter steht neben dir und stellt viele Fragen.

Du: (gratulierst Ryan zum Geburtstag)

____

Ryan: *Thanks. I'm having a great party. Sorry you can't be here.*
Mutter: Was spielen sie denn für Spiele?
Du: *Ryan, my mum wants to know something:*

What ____________________

____________________ ?
Ryan: *Well, we don't play games at my parties.*

Du: Ach, sie spielen bei ____________________

____

Ryan: *We're listening to music and singing along.*

Du: *I must tell my mum. She doesn't like music at parties.*
Mutter: Was machen sie denn?

Du: Sie ____________________

____

Ryan: *Why doesn't your mum like music?*

Du: Ryan möchte wissen, ____________________

____

Mutter: Weil deine Musik immer so laut ist.

Du: Ach! ____________________

____

5 Bei Mrs Brown (Unit 5)

Ein deutscher Junge und seine Mutter sind diese Woche bei Mrs Brown. Da seine Mutter kein Englisch spricht, muss der Junge beim Gespräch mit Mrs Brown die Fragen und Antworten vermitteln. Was sagt er? (Denke daran, dass es nur um die wesentlichen Informationen geht.)

Mother: Es gibt anscheinend keine Handtücher in meinem Zimmer. Bitte frage Mrs Brown – höflich natürlich –, ob sie welche für mich hat.

Boy: ______________________________

Mrs B.: *Oh, I'm sorry. Tell your mother the towels are in the little white cupboard in her room.*

Boy: ______________________________

____

Mother: Ach, so. Gut. Und ich wollte auch wissen, ab wann wir morgen frühstücken können. Wir sollten nicht zu spät aufstehen, weißt du. Wir wollen doch die Zeit hier gut ausnützen.

Boy: *What* ______________________________

Mrs B. *Oh, any time after half past seven. Do you want an English breakfast?*

Boy: ______________________________

____

Mother: Ja bitte. Wenn wir hier in England sind, wollen wir wie die Engländer leben.

Boy: ______________________________

6 Ferien auf dem Bauernhof (Unit 6)

Die englische Familie Down möchte eine Woche Ferien auf eurem Hof machen. Sie können aber nur ganz wenig Deutsch, also sollst du deiner Mutter bei der gegenseitigen Verständigung helfen.

Mutter: Sie wollen eine Woche bleiben, stimmt das?

Du: ______________________________

Mr Down: *Yes, that's correct. And have you got two rooms for us?*

Du: ______________________________

Mutter: Ja, das Doppelzimmer oben ist für die Eltern. Die Kinder haben das große Dreibettzimmer. Sag ihnen, dass es auch oben unterm Dach ist.

Du: ______________________________, *Mr and Mrs Down.*

____

____

Kim Down: *And can we feed the animals?*

Du: Sie möchte wissen, ob ______________________________

Mutter: Ja, natürlich. Du kannst den Kindern den Hof und die Tiere zeigen, und ich bringe die Eltern aufs Zimmer.

Du: *Come on, I can* ______________________________,

and my mother can ______________________________

7 Belina macht sich Sorgen (Unit 7)

Belina hat vor, an einer internationalen Musiksommerschule teilzunehmen. Sie findet zwar in Deutschland statt, aber in englischer Sprache. Belina spricht mit ihrem deutsch-amerikanischen Freund Matt darüber. Matt versteht Deutsch, aber er spricht immer Englisch.

Vervollständige den Dialog.

Matt: *The summer school's going to be great, Belina. You're going to meet lots of interesting people.*
Belina: Ja, aber sie werden alle Englisch sprechen.
Matt: *What's the matter? Your English is OK.*
Belina: Aber ich verstehe vielleicht nicht alles.

Matt: *Well, tell them and ask them to say it again. Just say,* "I'm sorry, I don't understand. ____________

____________"

Belina: Aber wenn sie zu schnell reden und ich nichts verstehe?

Matt: *Then say, "____________"*

Belina: Ja, das kann ich machen. Ich habe nur Angst, dass sie Wörter verwenden, die ich nicht kenne.
Matt: *Oh, Belina's a scaredy-cat!*
Belina: Was bin ich? Siehst du, das Wort kenne ich nicht.
Matt: *Come on, Belina. You know what "scared" means. Someone who is scared is a scaredy-cat.*
Belina: Ach so, ein Angsthase soll ich sein.
Matt: *You see. It's easy. If you don't know a word, you can ask about it. Say, "____________*

____________"

And if there's something you really don't understand, then ask them to use another phrase.

"____________

____________"

And when you understand that, don't forget to say thank you!

Belina: Das kann ich. *Thank you, Matt. It's going to be a great summer school!*

Seite 16 **1** 1. Who 2. Where 3. Who 4. What 5. Where 6. How **2** 1. six folders, two books and five comics (and four drawers); one school bag (and one desk). 2. In picture two there are two pencil cases, seven biros/pens, and four pencils. There are three rubbers, but there is only one ruler (and one desk). **3** Zeile 1: 4, 1, 3, 3; Z. 2: 2, 2, 2, 3 Z. 3: 4, 3, 2, 1

Seite 17 **4** 1. Where, your, it's, it's, its, You're 2. Where, We're 3. there, where, their, They're **5** 1. Hello, I'm Nina / Markus. I'm new here. 2. I'm from Augsburg in Germany / Germany. 3. I'm twelve. Are you in my tutor group? **6** 1. Where are we? – We're on page 17, exercise 6. 2. It's your turn. – No, it's their turn. 3. You're late, Mr Cooper. Where's your bag? 4. Where are Robert and David? – They're in their classroom.

Seite 26 **1** 2. Has David got a sister? – No, he hasn't. He's got a brother. 3. Have the Burtons got a swimming pool? – No, they haven't. They've got a garden. 4. Has Sarah got a horse? – No, she hasn't. She's got a cat. 5. Has Robert got a CD player? – Yes, he has. 6. Has Becky got a computer? – Yes, she has. **2** 2. a – an 3. an – a 4. an – a 5. a – an 6. a – an 7. an – a 8. a – an 9. an – a 10. a – an **3** 1. roof 2. tennis 3. bottle 4. afternoon 5. spoon 6. matter 7. little 8. swimming pool 9. tree 10. hall 11. door 12. bedroom 13. glass 14. call 15. need 16. Eddy 17. brilliant 18. funny 19. silly 20. Hill

Seite 27 **4** **a)** [f]: 1. knife 2. laugh 5. roof 8. funny [v]: 3. have 4. shelves 6. seven 7. knives **b)** [z]: 1. magazine 5. bags 6. lazy 7. roads [s]: 2. comics 3. parents 4. forks 8. cups **5** 2. Becky can't listen to the CD. 3. Robert can't play football. 4. Mark can write his name. 5. David can't draw a house. 6. Barker can play football. **6** *(Vorschläge)* 1. Can you go to the park with me? Sorry, I can't. I must go to the supermarket. 2. Can you play football with me? Sorry, I can't. I must go and see my grandma. 3. Can you go to the swimming pool with me? Sorry, I can't. I must do my homework. 4. Can you read a book with me? Sorry, I can't. I must set the table.

Seite 28 **1** 1. Has Kim got Sarah's CD? – No, she hasn't, but she's got her lunchbox. 2. Can Robert draw a horse? – No, he can't, but he can draw a cat. 3. Have the Burtons got a supermarket? No, they haven't, but they've got a bike shop. 4. Are the children in the classroom? – No, they aren't, but they're in the playground. 5. Has Becky got football posters in her room? – No, she hasn't, but she's got animal posters. **2** 1. There are two women in this picture, but there are four women in that picture. 2. There is one man in this picture, but there are seven men in that picture. 3. There is one girl in this picture, but there are three girls in that picture. **3** [ʌ]: but, must, under [ʊ]: full, put, foot [u:]: computer, spoon, tutor [ɜ:]: Burtons, hurt, turn

Seite 29 **4** 1. This – that 2. Those 3. These – those 4. This – that 5. these – those 6. This – that 7. These – those 8. those 9. This – that 10. these **5** 2. listen/say 3. lock 4. cup/saucer 5. children 6. horse/frog 7. breakfast 8. chair/desk 9. knee 10. skateboard 11. Indian/Italian **6** 1. Is it my turn? – No, it's the girls' turn. 2. Let's go together. – No, you go alone. 3. Can I come in? – No, sorry, I'm busy.

Seite 36 **1** 1. Simon is in the garden. He isn't playing with a ball. He's playing with Barker. 2. Sarah and Kim are in the living room. They aren't watching TV. They're watching a video. 3. Becky is in her room. She isn't reading comics. She's writing an e-mail. 4. Mr and Mrs Burton are at home. They aren't working. They're listening to music. 5. Jenny is outside. She isn't walking to the shops. She's waiting for the bus. **2** 1. wet – a 2. letter – e 3. driver – g 4. mobile – b 5. win – f 6. boyfriend – d 7. last – c

Seite 37 **3** They, it, We, them, her, us, you, your, you, it, My, he, his, him, he, us **4** *(Vorschläge)* 1. Thank you. 2. No, I've got them in my bag/pocket. 3. Yes, but you can take the bus./No it isn't. 4. It's the 13/… . 5. Let's go inside! 6. OK, let's go. 7. Great, we can buy some comics/… . 8. Sorry, he's not at home. 9. No, I'm OK, thank you. 10. Bye.

Seite 47 **1** **a)** 1. muesli 2. weekend 3. middle 4. England 5. rabbit 6. love 7. kitchen 8. pet **b)** 1. teatime 2. Wednesday (etc.) 3. always/never 4. classroom 5. skateboard/car 6. go 7. cinema/… 8. bush **2** I'm, live, is, rides, comes, am, is doing, am playing, are, are sitting, are looking, hates, shouts, is standing up, going, Go, shouts, love, looks after **3** *eigene Lösung*

Seite 48 **1** Zeile 1: castle, park, cinema; Z. 2: church, café, bookshop, shopping centre **2** **a)** Two boys are riding their scooters. A family is coming into the park. A man is drawing a picture. Three children are playing with a ball. A girl is taking a dog for a walk. **b)** The family is having a picnic now. The man isn't drawing. He is looking at his picture.The three children aren't playing with their ball. They are buying ice creams. The girl is calling her dog. **3** I, you, We, It, I, right, can, us, your, me, you, they/we, I, me

Seite 49 **4** 1. subject 2. zoo 3. wash 4. pound 5. uniform 6. buy 7. kindergarten 8. week 9. grandpa 10. pony. Star: Johnny Depp. **5** On Mondays the Brown sisters watch a video. On Tuesdays they ride their bikes. On Wednesdays they make dinner for their parents. On Thursdays they play the guitar. On Fridays they meet their friends. On Saturdays they go shopping. On Sundays they have lunch in a restaurant. **6** 2. Mrs Croft and Robert often go to the cinema on Saturdays, but this Saturday they're having dinner in a restaurant. 3. David usually plays the guitar on Monday evening, but this Monday evening he's riding Robert's scooter. 4. Jenny sometimes makes breakfast on Sunday morning, but this Sunday morning she's staying in bed. 5. The Burtons often go for picnics at the weekend, but this